the

minimalist mom

How to Simply Parent Your Baby

the minimalist mom

How to Simply Parent Your Baby

Rachel Jonat, Creator of TheMinimalistMom.com

Avon, Massachusetts

Published by
Adams Media, a division of F+W Media, Inc.
57 Littlefield Street, Avon, MA 02322. U.S.A.
www.adamsmedia.com

ISBN 10: 1-4405-9755-3
ISBN 13: 978-1-4405-9755-8
eISBN 10: 1-4405-9756-1
eISBN 13: 978-1-4405-9756-5

Printed in the United States of America.
10 9 8 7 6 5 4 3 2 1

Library of Congress Cataloging-in-Publication Data
Jonat, Rachel, author.
The minimalist mom: how to simply parent your baby / by Rachel Jonat.
Avon, Massachusetts: Adams Media, [2016]
LCCN 2016012632 | ISBN 9781440597558 (pob) | ISBN 1440597553 (pob) | ISBN 9781440597565 (ebook) | ISBN 1440597561 (ebook)
LCSH: Simplicity. | Families. | Child rearing. | Parenting. | Lifestyles. | BISAC: FAMILY & RELATIONSHIPS / Parenting / General. | FAMILY & RELATIONSHIPS / Life Stages / Infants & Toddlers.
LCC BJ1496.J663 2016 | DDC 649/.122--dc23
LC record available at *https://lccn.loc.gov/2016012632*

This book is intended as general information only, and should not be used to diagnose or treat any health condition. In light of the complex, individual, and specific nature of health problems, this book is not intended to replace professional medical advice. The ideas, procedures, and suggestions in this book are intended to supplement, not replace, the advice of a trained medical professional. Consult your physician before adopting any of the suggestions in this book, as well as about any condition that may require diagnosis or medical attention. The author and publisher disclaim any liability arising directly or indirectly from the use of this book.

Cover design by Frank Rivera.

This book is available at quantity discounts for bulk purchases.
For information, please call 1-800-289-0963.

Dedication

For my firstborn, Henry, who never liked the bouncer or
exersaucer or the activity mat. You were wise from the start.

Contents

Introduction

A four-bedroom house with a fenced-in yard. Three different strollers. Stuffed animals that sing, light up, and promise to make your three-month-old sleep through the night. A closet full of tiny, coordinated outfits. (With shoes.) Music and swim classes.

Oh, the massive amount of stuff that they say you need to buy and do for a new baby. Or do you?

It's time to cut through the avalanche of gear and activities and remember what's most important: quality time with your baby. How can you get more of that? With minimalist parenting. Resist the temptation to have more, do more, and buy more, and you'll find yourself feeling free. You'll have more money, less stress, and more time, thanks to your streamlined efficiencies. Being a minimalist parent gives you the time and energy to be more engaged with your kids, more intentional in your actions, and more focused on your family's happiness and well-being.

I know you can live with less because I do it with my family. My blog, *The Minimalist Mom* at *www.theminimalistmom.com/blog/,* started as a place for me to document my family's journey to a minimalist lifestyle. After my first son was born, I bought every gadget, swaddle, and toy in hopes that it would make my baby sleep more and bring some peace to our tired lives as parents of a newborn. None of it lived up to the promises on the box—and all of it created more for me to tidy, clean, and pay for. I was supposed to be enjoying parenthood and my beautiful new baby, but instead I was managing all the stuff accumulating in our home. Add in that we were in $80,000 of nonmortgage debt, and I was a very stressed-out new mom.

Then I heard about minimalism; about letting go of things and living smaller; having more time instead of buying more stuff. I didn't want to sell everything and live out of a backpack, but could I take the tenets of minimalism and apply them to my conventional life? I loved the idea of less, but I also loved having a couch and a dining room table, and even a few sweet but impractical outfits for my baby. I took the plunge and donated, sold, and recycled five carloads worth of housewares, electronics, clothing, and furniture. The result: less debt and stress and more time and space. We were out of nonmortgage debt in two short years. I felt less rushed, and it was easier to handle the inevitable and normal baby tears and rough sleep patches.

Since then, we've added two more children to our family. One of the best things we learned through minimalism is to forget about what other families are doing, or have, and instead zero in on what brings the best value and makes our life easiest. We have the money to hire great babysitters and the occasional cleaner because we don't buy a lot of things and we live in a small home with a modest mortgage payment. Minimalism continues to be one of the greatest gifts I have given both my family and myself.

This is a book about making the tough job of parenting easier by simplifying. Less stuff, more help. This is a book about being intentional about all that baby gear and not getting swept up in the tide of buying more new stuff at every turn. This is a book about figuring out what you really need instead of automatically buying what you can easily do without.

When you guard your space, money, and time when you have children, you'll simplify a lot of the challenges that new parents face. And when you make things simple, you make life a bit easier, a bit slower, and a lot more enjoyable.

What Is Minimalist Parenting?

In the tapestry of childhood, what stands out is not the splashy, blow-out trips to Disneyland but the common threads that run throughout and repeat: the family dinners, nature walks, reading together at bedtime, Saturday morning pancakes.

—*Kim John Payne*

Many of us live in houses that are larger than we actually need . . . yet it rarely seems that way. Why? Because we own so much stuff! People buy fives times as much clothing now as they did in the 1980s. Our homes are filled with gadgets, décor, abandoned art projects, forgotten sports equipment, and clothing we bought four years ago and still haven't worn. In short, we have a lot of stuff. Then, you have a baby and the amount of stuff seems to quadruple. Minimalist parenting is a way out of that never-ending quest to get more, bigger, larger.

The Problem with "More"

We have so much stuff because things are cheap and easy to acquire today. We have credit cards and same-day delivery, and it's all too easy to go to the store for a few things and bring home a cool stroller along with the bread and milk. We buy it thinking it will make life easier or more enjoyable, but does it? The more we buy, the more we have to pay for, clean up, repair, and maintain. That item we bought to entertain us or make life simpler ends up gathering dust or breaking or we lose interest and move on to the next new product that sells the same promise.

You can no longer pack all of your belongings, and your kids, in a covered wagon for a cross-country move; the idea of squeezing everything we own into a minivan or SUV is preposterous, and yet, that was once the norm. *More* is now convenient and cheap and the *answer* to struggles big and small. But *more* often just creates *more*: more work, more stress, more to look after, more to do, more to pay for, more to clean. Unless we're talking about free and fantastic childcare, *more* certainly doesn't make parenting a new baby easier.

Benefits of Minimalist Parenting

This book is about making life easier when you have a new baby. *Easier,* when you have a tiny being to take care of, is about simplifying your schedule, home, and lifestyle as much as possible. Minimalist parenting is about removing things you don't need—extra payments, clutter, an overscheduled social calendar—and enjoying the money, time, and space they leave behind.

There are myriad reasons to adopt principles of minimalist parenting. Here are some of the most rewarding benefits.

More Intentional Parenting

So much of parental stress and its outcroppings (limited patience, shouting matches you later regret, tardiness, and so on) arise from having too much stuff in your house and too many places to go. When you remove some of those obstacles (by decluttering your house or removing a few obligations from your calendar), your parenting style can align with your intentions. No parent enjoys battling for a clean playroom, so make that battle easier by putting less in the playroom to begin with. When you live with less, your parenting techniques and behavior will change too.

Better Financial Outlook

When you live with less, you save money. It's that simple. Turn an underused room into a nursery; buy a swing that's also a bouncy seat and does double the work; take a free baby music class at your local library instead of the pricey, private place across town. These choices all affect your family's bottom line.

Less Stress

The more you have going on in your life, the more you have to worry about. How will you ever keep your four-bedroom house clean? How can you make it from work to 6 P.M. daycare pickup with all this traffic? Is your baby awake at 3 A.M. because his swaddle isn't comfortable enough? Should you try one of the other six swaddles you have instead?

The list is endless. Simplify your life and you'll reduce stress. You won't be juggling as many things, and you'll learn that not all the balls have to be in the air at once to raise a happy family.

Confidence in Your Choices

Should we try to go on a big vacation like our neighbors just did? Do we really need a big SUV once the baby arrives? Is the small second bedroom too small for a baby? You'll face dozens of questions as you enter parenthood. Minimalist parenting gives you a philosophy to guide you and the confidence to make decisions that are best for your life and your family.

No more worries about what your friends are doing or what your parents say when you tell them you've decided to use a portable crib in the corner of your master bedroom instead of outfitting and decorating a nursery. Deciding to live with less stuff, to prioritize your time over things, offers a new level of contentment and easy answers when people inevitably offer advice or question your choices.

More Free Time

Time is finite and nothing makes that clearer than adding a baby to your family. Adopting some minimalist parenting tactics can actually give you more time in your day. That's more time for your baby, for yourself, and for your spouse. Instead of spending your evenings sorting baby clothing, or cleaning up a sea of toys, you can give that time to what really matters to you: family, hobbies, your career, or more sleep!

Use Minimalist Parenting to Align Your Life with Your Values

One tenet of minimalist parenting is to really think about where you are devoting your time, money, and space. Often, our values aren't in alignment with our actions, and that imbalance creates more stress in your life.

What do you value most? The first answer people often give to this question is family. Saying you value family is an easy answer, of course, but is it really what you value most in your actions? If you value family above all, how do you align that value with how you spend your time and money? A person who values their family above all may spend more on housing so that she can live closer to her job, saving her an hour of commute time each day. Then, she can spend that hour with her family—eating dinner together, playing a board game, reading a bedtime story. Unfortunately, many of us make different choices—ones that aren't in line with valuing family above all else.

If you value health, do you work four days a week instead of five, taking a pay cut and living simply, so that you can train for an Ironman triathlon? If education is a big priority for you, do you contribute to an education savings plan for your children and volunteer at a local high school as a tutor?

Take some time to think about what you value and how you spend your time and money on these things. It can be a tough question. We may often look through our cash outflow and see that most of what we spend is on housing, transportation, and stuff. We may look through our time and see that our week is mostly made up of long days at work with time in the car and evenings spent watching television. The hobbies or passions that align with our values are just random blips on the few weekends that aren't stolen by housework or catching up on projects for the day job. Minimalism helps your values reclaim their top spot in your life. When you have more time, money, and space to devote to the things you love most, you'll find yourself happier and more fulfilled.

Make a Values List

Make a list of your values and identify the time and money you invest in them. It could look as simple as the following two examples.

Value List Example #1

- **Career.** I'm investing tuition, money, and time to take a project management certification course that will make me a candidate for advancement.
- **Time outdoors.** I spend weekends skiing and take camping vacations.
- **Nutrition.** I buy organic produce and locally raised meat. I rarely eat out and mostly cook at home.

Value List Example #2

- **Family.** I'm using savings to extend my parental leave and recently took a job with a four-day workweek, and a pay cut, so I could help my aging parents more.
- **House.** We purchased a fixer-upper in a neighborhood we love and spend a lot of our weekends, and money, renovating it.
- **Reading and books.** I have a big library in my home, buy several new books a month, and spend a lot of my free time reading.

It's easy to let your values be obscured by the dominant values in your social circle or community. You may value work freedom above all else but end up turning down that flexible work-from-home job because you feel the pressure to be in a well-paid career-advancing job. You may value community engagement and volunteering, but once you moved to the suburbs, you just couldn't participate in that teen mentoring program that met in the city once a week. If you highly value something, it should show in how you align your living and spending so you can support and do that very thing.

Aligning Values and Parenting

New parents usually have a harsh and fast indoctrination in spending time and money that align with their values. After a few nights of very little sleep, they realize that above all, above watching another episode of a television show, socializing, or even having a newly remodeled kitchen, they will spend and do whatever they need to for six uninterrupted hours of sleep.

This is not a call to deprive yourself of every luxury, big and small, but rather to rethink those luxuries and pick out the ones that give you the best value for your time and money. So perhaps you purchase the fancy coffee only twice a week because you really value your relationship and want to hire a babysitter once a month to go out on a date.

There is often a burst of motivation and will when a first child is born. I will never eat fast food again. I will give up that occasional cigarette for good. I will start eating a proper breakfast instead of a PowerBar and coffee on the train into work. New parents may find themselves overwhelmed with motivation to take better care of themselves, to save more money so they can provide for this new bundle down the road, and they may even give up some of their more selfish hobbies in order to be present and engaged parents. Parenthood can inspire big changes to align your resource spending with your values: use that motivation. It may not be the right time to, say, move you and your four-week-old baby from the city to the country to start an organic dairy farm, but it could be the right time to start tracking finances, sticking to a budget, or getting into the habit of eating dinner with your spouse every night.

What Type of Minimalist Parent Are You?

Becoming a minimalist parent isn't an all-or-nothing venture— you can approach it in degrees and customize your choices based on your family's needs, location, and preferences. To help you decide how to tailor your approach, I'll show you three types of minimalist families throughout the book: Beginner, Intermediate, and All-In. Each one practices minimalism, just in varying degrees.

- **Beginner:** The Beginner minimalist family is starting to dabble in some low-risk minimalism. They've adopted a few simple living hacks that can give them more time and save them some money. For example, they might purchase most of their baby gear new, but look for secondhand versions of a couple of high-cost items. They aren't ready to downsize their living space, but they declutter and prioritize only the baby gear items they truly need to keep their home streamlined.

- **Intermediate:** This minimalist family has taken some significant steps to living more simply. At times, they still like to indulge in spots they've prioritized. They may have taken on one more radical thing, like going without a car or staying with the baby in their one-bedroom with den apartment, but they also enjoy some luxuries, like a premium stroller and hiring some extra help for weeks after the baby arrives.
- **All-In:** As the name implies, the All-In family embraces as many facets of minimalism as possible. They may have a big end goal in mind, like early retirement, or they may live in a city with a very high cost of living. This all-in tactic could also be a temporary approach to slashing debt or living off one income while a spouse is finishing school.

Throughout the book, you'll see how each family approaches some of the major decisions, such as living space, baby gear, clothes, and time management. You might find that one of these family types closely matches all of your preferences, or you might find that you're a Beginner when it comes to housing but All-In when it comes to gear. Any approach will work! Do what works best for your family. Any and all steps you take toward living simpler will pay off. Let's get started.

Home

The question of what you want
to own is the question of how
you want to live your life.

—Marie Kondo

If you're feeling the pressure to upsize your home before the baby arrives, resist. You don't have to commit to your small space forever, but with some creativity and a bit of decluttering, most families can make their small home livable for many years. In this chapter, we will examine how to rightsize your home and its contents to make life easier with a young baby. We will look at several different home and lifestyle choices and how to maximize simplicity, whether you live in a 3,000-square-foot home or a 600-square-foot apartment. Sometimes the easiest way to rightsize is to stay right where you are and maximize the space you have, so you'll learn some easy ways to declutter your home before the baby arrives. We'll also tackle baby's room—how much space do you really need for a nursery (actually, do you need one at all?), and how should you furnish it? Get ready to think differently about your living space from top to bottom.

Leave your preconceived ideas of what a family home looks like behind in this chapter. Open your mind to think a bit differently: the rewards—time, money, even sleep—are too big not to. First, let's discuss what a substantial impact your housing costs have on your life and finances.

Rightsize Your Home

There is often a big push to upsize your housing as soon as you know you're pregnant. While your parents' generation may have seen buying a house as a step toward *having it all*, or required before having children, that simply isn't the case today. Many cities have changed dramatically since your parents' early adulthood. What was once an affordable starter home could now be a teeth-gnashing, panic-inducing stretch for the student loan–ridden university graduate in the early stretch of his or her career. The cool kids are no longer buying the big new car with a big new lease payment or loan. The cool kids are buying a used car with mostly cash or moving closer to a spouse's job so they can be a one-car family. The cool kids are looking into the "tiny house" movement. You are not living in your parents' economy or culture, so stop measuring your success against their old measures and ideas. Owning big, expensive things is not a hallmark of adulthood.

> **Tip**
>
> Enlarging your living space also equals increased cost. The moving process alone is expensive in so many ways: Realtor fees, mortgage discharge fees, moving fees, and then, of course, there's the actual increased cost of a bigger home and bigger mortgage and interest. If you can stay in your current home instead of upsizing, all that money will be back in your pocket. (Plus, you won't lose several weekends and evenings devoted to packing and unpacking!)

In fact, big homes, those above 1,200 square feet, are relatively new. According to the National Association of Home Builders (NAHB), in the 1950s, the average home was only 983 square feet!

How Much Space Do You Really Need?

It's true; you may eventually want to move into something bigger, but why not wait until you really need to? Babies and toddlers, and really most children eight years old and under, are small. They don't actually take up that much physical space.

When people say they need to move because the kids need more space, it's often not the children who need more space; it's the stuff. Most people add 30 percent more stuff to their home with each additional child. So those children, the ones that arrive at a mere seven or eight pounds, are not actually taking up that much space. It's all their stuff that takes up space.

Before you immediately assume you need to move, consider how much space you truly need. Instead of thinking about using a room for one activity—sleeping, eating, playing—think about making a room work for you for the maximum number of hours. The minimalist home gives rooms two or more functions, so you can do more in less space. To start rightsizing your space, write out your weekly schedule and then list each room in your home. Write down how many hours a week each room is used. Here's a sample list of room and time usage for a family with two working parents, an older child who goes to bed around the same time as the parents, and a younger child with an earlier bedtime. Like most families, they spend a lot of time together in their living room, and the younger child plays with toys in her bedroom on the weekend. They live in an average (for our times) four-bedroom and den home.

Sample Weekly Family Space Usage by Hour in a Four-Bedroom Home

- Master Bedroom: 60 hours
- Child Bedroom #1: 60 hours
- Child Bedroom #2: 70 hours
- Guest Bedroom: 0 hours
- Den: 8 hours
- Living Room: 34 hours
- Dining Room: 14 hours
- Kitchen: 16 hours
- Total possible weekly hours for the home (eight rooms x 156 hours): 1,248
- Total actual weekly use: 262 hours
- Total unused room time per week: 986 hours

That's a lot of time for rooms to sit empty. Some of this is unavoidable: most people don't want to sleep in their kitchens as a space saver, or they never leave their houses. But efficiencies could be made and a lot of savings could be earned in the first model. Let's see what life would like for this family in a two-bedroom apartment with an open concept dining/living room and a small desk in the master bedroom that could be used as an office.

Sample Weekly Family Space Usage by Hour in a Two-Bedroom Apartment

- Master Bedroom: 68 hours
- Second Bedroom: 70 hours
- Living/Dining Room: 48 hours
- Kitchen: 16 hours
- Total possible weekly hours for the home (four rooms x 156 hours): 624 hours
- Total actual weekly use: 262 hours
- Total weekly-unused room time: 362 hours

In the first model, the family uses just under 21 percent of their room hours each week; in the second model, they use almost 42 percent of their room hours. Now, downsizing radically from a 2,400-square-foot home to a 1,200-square-foot apartment may not be your end goal, but one big takeaway from this time and home use exercise is to see how little we actually use our homes. We're paying for all that space every minute of the day, even if we're away on vacation or just having a normal week at the office.

Here's another vote for living smaller: life with small kids is easier when they are within reach and earshot. That large house with four sets of stairs is going to be a lot of work with a newborn who wakes up every two hours, a crawling baby, or toddler. You'll be exhausted from running all over that house.

The Financial Benefits of Staying Small

One of the biggest expenses for growing a family is housing. The U.S. Department of Agriculture (USDA) says that housing comprises 30 percent of the overall cost of raising a child. The USDA estimates that a child born in 2013 to a middle-income couple will cost $245,000. That's $73,500 on increased housing for one child. Add a second child and you're looking at almost $150,000 on increased housing. Increased housing costs are a considerable part of the cost of raising children . . . but do they have to be? We're going to examine ways that minimalism can cut this cost and how you could think a bit differently and act a bit differently to save yourself a lot of money and time.

If you can manage in a small home for a few extra years, or forever, you can reap big savings, including:

- Reduced/stabilized rent or mortgage
- Smaller heating bills
- Less time cleaning
- Less furniture and décor bought to fill a bigger space

- Less money spent on conveniences you might be able to avoid—for example, you might not need to buy a baby monitor if your baby's room is very close to your own

That doesn't even count your smaller environmental footprint! If you like to work in hard numbers, consider where your savings would be realized. For example, one less hour a week of cleaning is like giving yourself an extra week of vacation each year. If you're paying someone $20 an hour to clean your home, taking an hour off the cleaning bill each week is over $1,000 saved every year.

By the Numbers

Here are some examples of how to save money by living in a smaller home and having a shorter commute. Relate these models to your own lifestyle and look for ways that you could live smaller to save more.

Family One: Is expecting their first child and currently lives in a two-bedroom apartment they rent for $1,000 a month. They are thinking about renting a house further outside the city for $1,500 a month, but it would also mean getting a second car, which they estimate will be another $400/month. What if they made that two-bedroom apartment work until their first child was five years old?

- No second car for five years: savings of $24,000.
- No larger rent payment for five years: savings of $30,000.

- By staying in a smaller home until their child is school age, Family One could save $54,000.

Think of what they could do with that money. They could vacation, retire sooner, give more to charity, have more disposable income for babysitters, yoga classes, or other activities and services they find rewarding. Perhaps they could even use that money as a down payment for a home.

Family Two: Expecting their second and likely final child, they currently own a three-bedroom bungalow. They would like to move into something bigger with more of a yard and an updated kitchen. When they look at moving into a bigger and more expensive home, they will extend their mortgage by another five years, will increase their payment by $600/month, and will pay $8,000 in closing costs and for more furniture for this bigger home. They also estimate their utilities will increase by $50/month and they will hire someone to keep the lawn and garden for $100/month. What if they made the bungalow work until child number two was 18 years old?

- No $600 mortgage increase: $129,600.
- No moving and closing costs or new furniture to buy: $8,000.
- No increase in utilities and no lawn maintenance needed: $32,400.

If Family Two stayed in their current home, they would be mortgage-free five years earlier and save $170,000. That's an incredible amount of money for simply deciding not to upgrade their home.

> **Tip**
>
> We haven't even factored compound interest into these calculations. The actual numbers would be even higher if you invested those extra dollars each month, or used them to pay off a mortgage faster. Deciding to enjoy where you live right now could be a bold move, not only for simplifying your life but also for your financial future.

Imagine a Brighter Financial Future

Clearly, living smaller and resisting the call to go bigger and better can help you realize huge savings—enough to really change the course of your life. You could:

- Retire earlier
- Be able to take a one-year sabbatical from work while your children are still at home
- Have more money for travel
- Give more money to your favorite causes
- Alleviate some of your financial distress (getting out of your current mortgage earlier, paying off college debts or car loans, etc.)
- Save more money for your children's college educations, weddings, or first homes

These goals are all attainable if you consider living smaller now. Yet this simple idea of living a bit smaller, or below your means, is actually quite radical. Conventional measures of success are often what you drive, where you live, and what your salary is. We think we should be lusting after everything new, upgrading our cell phones and our cars, and moving to more expensive neighborhoods as soon as we can get approved for financing. Once you hit one level of luxury or comfort, you should be going after the next one. But there is no end game to this drive for more and better. The more you get, the more you want.

Wouldn't it be refreshing and enjoyable to decide to be content with what you already have? Step off the get more *want more* treadmill and, instead, see that you have enough. If you have a roof over your head, running water, and food in the fridge, you're richer than most of the world. Shake off the mind trap of wanting more and, instead, focus on the things you have that don't come with a receipt—like that new baby.

Repurpose Areas of Your Home to Find Extra Square Footage

One of the big reasons families move is because they want more space. What if you could get *more* space by multipurposing your existing space at various times of the day? Thinking creatively can increase your space—no move and no renovation required. For example, you could:

● Use your master bedroom for a nighttime sleeping space and a daytime playroom or office.

- Find kids' bunk beds that fold into the wall each morning to open up more space to play.
- Use your guest bedroom as an office and a nursery.
- Create a mobile nursery. Think about that: a door-width crib on wheels and a few baskets of baby clothing could be moved around your home to create a sleeping space for the baby almost anywhere.
- Put your toy box on wheels and roll it out into your open concept kitchen and dining area so the baby can play while you're working in the kitchen or even while you have friends over for a meal.
- Make your television and gaming equipment mobile by putting them on a rolling cart. This opens up your living room as an early bedtime spot for the baby or as a guest bedroom for the jetlagged visitor who needs sleep. For a large gathering, you can roll the cart into your master bedroom and create a second entertaining space for the older kids to watch a movie as they lounge on your bed.
- Use bench storage and collapsing chairs to turn your three-season porch into a year-round hosting area, play area, and craft room. Winter weekends can be spent with the chairs folded and out of the way, the table moved to one side for a craft project, and the floor space used for toddlers burning up some energy on ride-on toys. A few quick moves of furniture and you can be entertaining friends in the same space after the kids have gone to bed.

- Put all of your plastic storage containers, bowls, and light pots and pans in low kitchen cabinets and drawers for easy entertainment for older babies and toddlers. Yes, the original home multitasker was letting babies safely explore and entertain themselves with kitchen items. No playroom or toys required!

- Have a mix of plush and lightweight dining room seating and an extendable dining table to maximize space and use. Keep the table in its smaller size for everyday use, and use extra chairs throughout the home as needed: a plush chair in the kid's room to read books in, a lightweight chair with the desk in the office/guest bedroom, a plush chair as seating in the living room. When you have a large gathering, collect chairs from other rooms. This tactic eliminates having all those chairs that only get used once a year and a table that seats ten—when you're a family of four— eating up space. Yet you can still easily host Thanksgiving dinner or throw a big dinner party.

Parents Who've Done It

These ideas may seem radical, but parents everywhere are using them successfully every day. Joanna Goddard, writer of the lifestyle blog *A Cup of Jo* at *www.cupofjo.com*, turned a bathroom into the baby's sleeping space in her New York apartment. Joanna's apartment had two bedrooms and two bathrooms, and their older son was in one bedroom and the parents had the other. They needed a quiet room for their second child to sleep in, and one of the bathrooms was large enough to accommodate a small portable crib. Voilà—the second bathroom was used for its primary purpose for twelve hours a day and turned into a third bedroom for the other twelve hours a day.

Adrian Crook, father of five and blogger at *5 Kids 1 Condo* at *www.5kids1condo.com*, turned his master bedroom into a room that works as an office during the day, an entertainment area and playroom for kids in the evening and on weekends, and a sleeping space overnight. He had his queen-size bed converted to a Murphy-style bed with a desk attachment, opening up the room for use in the daytime. The Crook family's master bedroom is now used up to twenty-four hours a day instead of the usual eight hours.

Maximize Space by Decluttering

Here's one way to prepare for a new baby that isn't in any guide for new parents: get rid of things you aren't using. Decluttering and clearing out your rarely or never-used home goods, clothing, and *stuff* is an easy almost no-cost, or sometimes even cash-generating, way to prepare for parenthood—and create more room in your home. Having fewer things will also leave you with less to clean and maintain when the baby arrives.

Paring down will also make you enjoy what you do have more. Many people can't find and use those nice things they do have simply because their other stuff is taking up too much space. One of the best rewards of decluttering is using the things you really enjoy more: the dress you've been saving for a special occasion will be worn at date night, the vase you think is too precious to have out can now be enjoyed every day, and that special olive oil a friend brought back from Italy can be part of a Friday night meal.

Decluttering, Room by Room

Pregnancy may not be the best time to move everything out of the attic or finally empty the garage. Instead, take a slow and steady approach for some quick and easy decluttering wins. Set aside a few hours a week to work through the clutter hot spots listed below. It could be as short as thirty minutes every evening or an afternoon each weekend. If you find yourself stuck in one area, leave it and move on to another. If you're halfway done as your due date approaches, congratulate yourself on what you have accomplished and save the rest for when you're well and rested and settled into your new routine as a parent.

Kitchen
- Clean out expired items from the pantry and donate anything you bought on a whim that you know you won't use in the next year.
- Scale down your water glass and mug collection to just what will fit in the top rack of your dishwasher.
- Donate duplicate kitchen utensils and cookware.

Books
- Trim your book collection to just what you will read again or would loan to a friend. (Yes, the college textbooks and your bridal magazine collection can go!)

Clothes

- If you're in maternity wear, pack your nonfitting *regular* clothes into boxes. As you do that, weed out those items you haven't worn in a few years for donation.

- Keep your early-stage pregnancy garments handy for the postbaby stage.

Paper

- Look through your filed items for old statements that can be shredded.

- Get rid of warranties and receipts for items that you no longer own or that the warranty has now expired.

- Move as many statements to paperless or e-statements as possible.

Electronics and Media

- If you're not watching DVD-format movies anymore, don't keep them. Find a pawnshop that will buy your DVDs or donate them to your local library.

- Old electronics, like cell phones and cameras, should be recycled with any data removed.

Sporting Goods

- If you haven't skied in ten years, you are unlikely to start again once you have a newborn. Sell your unused sports equipment and put that money into an account for now. If you get the itch and time, you can start back up with rented equipment or buy second-hand again with the money from that account.

Miscellaneous Stuff

- Any home will have a few drawers and closets filled with other items, like home décor and gadgets and that piece of furniture you were going to decoupage or use chalk paint on. If you haven't touched it in a few years, if you haven't finished that craft project you started almost a year ago, if it's cluttering up your spare room and you feel guilty every time you walk by it, let it go. You have a new exciting project coming up: a baby.
- When life gets slower, you can get back into smaller craft projects, visit a crafting studio, or use craft time as a social hour and pool your pared-down resources with your friends' at a craft night.

Making your home easier to function in and clean is a great gift to give yourself before you become a parent. Think of every box you send to donations, or every handbag you sell, as time and money you are giving yourself in the future. Future You will be so thankful to Present You for emptying the front hall closet, dealing with that pile of unsorted mail, and selling off those old bridesmaids' dresses. Having less to organize, sort, and stress over will give you more mental and physical space to enjoy parenthood, and you will have more time for yourself and your baby.

Downsizing

If you already live in a large space, a more radical option is to downsize as you start your family. Clearly, this unconventional choice will raise quite a few eyebrows as you share your decision with others. But if you've decided to embrace minimalism, it could be the best decision for you and your family—and that's what's most important.

Once you've decided, perhaps the biggest obstacle, besides selling your large home, is dealing with the social backlash you might face (when people inevitably ask if you're out of your mind). Here are some ways to answer their questions:

- "We reassessed our priorities and decided that higher housing costs weren't the best way to spend our money as we raise a family."
- "Moving into a smaller house will allow us the financial freedom for one of us to stay home with our children while they're young."
- "Our choice isn't for everyone! But we're excited about what it means for our family and our financial future."

Chances are, the doubters will be converted when they see your enviable turn in finances with significant reduction in rent or mortgage payments and your new abundance of spare time now that weekends aren't tied up with cleaning and repairing a large home.

Nurseries: Big or Small or None

Once you've seen the pictures in magazines or Pinterest at *www.pinterest.com*, it's easy to want to blow out your budget on a nursery. You want the full, matching, fresh from the store 4-in-1 crib, dresser, changing table, and rocker. You also want a soft rug that matches your chosen theme, curtains, and some whimsical personalized art handcrafted just for your baby.

If you've been dreaming of the day you would walk into Pottery Barn and order a three-piece furniture set (which costs three times as much as your first car), let's talk. Let's hash out your dreams and wants vs. your needs. Let's find a place in the middle, one you will love and be proud of, but that will also keep your finances in check and give you some savvy shopping chops that will come in handy down the road.

Nurseries Cost How Much?!

All that nursery gear sure looks sweet, but break out the calculator—this dream is going to cost you. A report in Britain said new parents were spending almost £4,000—that's roughly $6,000—on new nurseries.

Is an expensive nursery worth the cost to you? Six thousand dollars is a lot of money to most people. There's a lot you could do with $6,000 that could have a greater impact on your life than a pretty room for an infant that can't appreciate it. With $6,000, you could:

- **Take extra parental leave.** Depending on your salary and employer, $6,000 could give you a few more weeks or even months with your baby.
- **Save for college.** Tuition rates are skyrocketing. Wouldn't it be great to know you have the first year of tuition saved before the baby was even born?
- **Put that money toward your mortgage.** Paying your mortgage off four months earlier may not seem like a big deal right now, but when you're in your fifties or sixties, it could mean extra months on the golf course, traveling, or just enjoying life with no job.
- **Take a trip.** Skip the nursery and go to Paris or Tokyo while you're on parental leave. Knock off one of your bucket list destinations with baby along.

> ### Tip
> Babies less than five months of age can be wonderful travel mates. They aren't usually mobile and still sleep a lot during the day. They aren't on solids yet, so there's less to pack.
>
> You can walk the Marais district with *bébé* along in a carrier or tuck into a fabulous lunch at a sidewalk café while junior snoozes next to you in a stroller.

Here's a Minimalism Secret: You Don't Really Need a Nursery

In the 1950s, a third of the babies had no nursery of their own. They shared a room with a sibling or parent. It wasn't until recent generations that babies started getting their own rooms. Historically, and currently in many places around the globe, babies slept in the same rooms as a parent or sibling. Your great-grandparents turned out just fine and they probably didn't have their own room as a baby. Your relatives a few generations back possibly would have laughed at the idea of a separate room for one baby.

> **Tip**
> If you're minimalist at heart, the idea of filling a whole room with baby gear might turn you off. There's nothing wrong with that feeling!

Tiny-apartment dwellers have babies just like people who live in six-bedroom houses. They really do. And those babies grow up just fine in a small home. Babies have been growing up in small apartments in New York City and in other big cities the world over for generations with no ill effect. Families in expensive cities, like New York and London, have had babies bunk in with parents for a long time, and they've made creative use of their small space. Even if you have the space, you could decide to keep a crib in your guest room or office instead of giving over an entire room to the baby and nursery furniture. Young babies will not know the difference between being in a room with your treadmill or in a room with matching wallpaper, rug, glider, artwork, and crib bedding.

But Where Will Baby Go?

If you live in a small home, you may already be considering the idea of skipping the nursery to save space. After all, babies are small. They really don't need a lot of dedicated space just for them. You nursery could be a den, a corner of your master bedroom, or a closet. Here are some creative ways to give your baby space to sleep and play without having her own nursery:

- Put a bassinet in your bedroom, and when the baby grows out of that, put a secondhand crib in your den.
- Change diapers on your bed or on the floor with a receiving blanket as a changing mat.
- Clear out a drawer in your dresser for baby clothes.
- Lay a quilt on the living room floor for the baby to roll around on.
- Buy a mini crib on wheels and move it around—into a walk-in closet at naptime, in the master bedroom when the baby first goes to sleep, then out to the living room when it's time for the parents to go to bed.

Tip

If you're in a one-bedroom apartment but really want a nursery, think about giving the baby the bedroom. You could use a foldout couch or Murphy bed in your living room and some creative storage to create two bedrooms. This is a common setup in high-cost-of-living cities, like San Francisco and New York.

Nursery Planning Questions

Before you buy any furniture or put up elephant wallpaper in the den, ask yourself some questions about how and when you plan to use your nursery.

- How much will we use this room? Will a parent be on parental leave for a long time, and does he or she expect to be at home and with the baby in that room for significant stretches of the day?
- Will a nanny or caregiver use this room a lot, or will our baby go to a daycare?
- Is it convenient to be in or get to the room while doing other household tasks, like laundry and cooking?
- Is it close enough to the parent's bedroom that walking to it every two hours at night won't be extra inconvenient?
- How much will we spend on the nursery, and what other things could we do with that money (like pay off student loans, take more parental leave, save more, or travel)?
- Are there ways we could save money and buy less for the nursery?

These questions will help you assess what you really need for your baby. Once you determine those needs, you can approach the nursery question from a realistic place, not a dream based on a magazine picture.

Nursery Furniture

Here's some news for a lot of first-time parents: many nurseries don't get used much. Why? You end up bringing a portable crib into your room for easier nighttime feeding. (Parents soon find that getting out of bed and going down the hall, or upstairs, multiple times a night is very disruptive to their sleep. A baby in arm's reach is much easier to tend to than a baby who's down the hall.) During the day, baby might fall asleep in a car seat while you're running errands. That's more missed time in the nursery itself. Or perhaps your baby will spend most days in a daycare center.

What does all this light or nonexistent use of nursery furniture mean for you? Deals. Before you drop hundreds or thousands of dollars on nursery furniture, check your local buy and sell forums. Many parents end up selling their $3,000 nursery for a few hundred dollars after barely using it. You will see lots of ads for an *almost new crib* with the description being *baby ended up sleeping with us*. Look on craigslist at *www.craigslist .org* or ask a local parent about buy and sell Facebook groups at *www.facebook.com* in your area to hunt down your nursery set.

Tips for Buying Secondhand Nursery Furniture

If the budget is small or nonexistent, and you really want nursery furniture, start asking around. If you're low on cash for a nursery, don't worry. Low on cash doesn't mean low on love. Many parents are all too happy to give away furniture, baby gear, and clothing once they are finally out of the baby stage. If you're able to pick up, and maybe even dismantle, a dresser or changing table, many people would be happy to hand their nursery furniture over to you for free. You can also find free furniture by:

- Look on The Freecycle Network at *www.freecycle.org* and post an ad for what you are looking for.
- Bookmark the free stuff section on craigslist at *www.craigslist.org* and set up an alert for furniture postings.
- Post an ad on a local buy and sell board.
- Check to see if you have something to barter. For example, if you have skills or something valuable you can trade—such as website design services, book-keeping or accounting or tax help, photography sessions, yoga classes—offer it up in exchange for nursery furniture. Bartering is making a comeback, and people are exchanging haircuts for homegrown apples and couches for an oil change. It's a wonderful cash-free system for selling and buying.
- Swap items you don't use for nursery furniture. Check out Yerdle at *www.yerdle.com*, the app that lets you buy and sell without exchanging money. You could turn all that unused sports gear in your garage, or that food processor you got as a wedding gift and have never used, into a crib or dresser for the baby's room.
- Search Facebook for a local Buy Nothing group. You can also check them out and find a group at *buynothingproject.org/find-a-group/.* These groups

work as a place for people to connect to get rid of items they no longer need and have other members take them off their hands. Once you are a member of the group, you can post In Search Of nursery furniture and list what you are looking for. It's helpful to include if you are able to transport items yourself, as well as how soon you can pick them up.

Whether you find what you want free, or have to pay a small amount for it, here are some things to look for when acquiring secondhand nursery furniture:

- **Bite marks on crib rails:** Usually these are just cosmetic, and if they don't bother you, use them to negotiate the price down significantly. Otherwise, keep looking.
- **Stained mattresses:** If a mattress is fairly new and has had a mattress protector on it, it should look fresh and smell fresh.
- **Manufacture date and serial number:** Bring a mobile device with you and look up manufacture dates by the item's serial number. If you know how old the piece is, you can either say no thank you, or you can negotiate the price down. Many people will downplay the age of an item, sometimes because they are the second owner of the crib.
- **Drop-side cribs and recalls:** Another reason to look up the serial number of a crib is to find out if it is a drop-side crib or if it has been recalled. Not every

drop-side crib has been recalled, but in December of 2010, new crib safety standards in the United States were approved that effectively banned drop-side cribs. As of June of 2011, drop-side cribs can no longer be manufactured or sold in the United States. Some manufacturers provide kits to convert drop-side cribs so the drop-down side does not move. Before you buy a used crib, figure out when the crib was manufactured and whether it has a drop-down side or is a drop-side.

● **Stains or tears on gliders:** Check seat cushions for stains and look for models with removable covers that you can wash. Always sit in the seat and check the rocking mechanism for squeaks and any catching. If possible, turn the chair over and look at the underside of the seat for broken springs or upholstery tears. Again, find the serial number and check online for the date of manufacture.

Create a Cool Look with Mismatched Furniture

Mismatched, midcentury modern, boho, and upcycled furniture are all very on-trend these days. Browse through Pinterest at *www.pinterest.com*, or the latest decorating magazine, and you'll see lots of nurseries with upcycled garage-sale finds or repurposed items. Secondhand is stylish! Consider collecting your crib, changing table, dresser, glider, and anything else from a few different places. It may not be as easy to source it all as it would be to just walk into one store and order everything, but it will cost considerably less money, be better for the earth, and still very stylish.

Soft Furnishings: Rugs, Pillows, and Bedding

Before you go out and buy a set of matching crib bedding and décor, consider these options:

- **Keep the décor minimal.** The American Academy of Pediatrics (AAP) warns against crib bumper use because of suffocation risks, so skip those and opt for a fair priced decorative crib sheet. The AAP also says that for babies under a year of age, you should avoid putting stuffed toys, pillows, quilts, and comforters in cribs—not buying those will save you a bundle and keep the crib neat and clean.
- **Sew your own matching crib skirts and sheets.** If you're not crafty, you could work with a family member who is—it could be their baby gift!
- **Keep in mind that the rug might suffer from formula spills, diaper blowouts, and spit up.** Find one that's easy to clean and/or not too costly to replace if necessary.

Buying all the owl-themed nursery accessories at a store like Pottery Barn could be a mortgage payment or two months of daycare costs, so these options are worth considering.

Artwork and Décor

You don't need to fill each wall with framed decorations. Babies can't see well at first anyway. Plus, there are so many options for homemade artwork or low-cost options that fit with minimalist goals.

- Think of what you already own. For example, if you have a family heirloom quilt in the attic, clean it and hang it on the wall for inexpensive and meaningful visual interest.
- Artists on Etsy at *www.etsy.com* offer prints that you download for a small fee and print and frame yourself.
- If you, or a loved one, have artistic inclinations, consider drawing or painting something to hang in the nursery.
- Maternity or other family photos in simple frames make a lovely addition to the wall of your baby's room.

You Don't Need Everything

What do you really need in a nursery? Not much. A place to sleep and something to store clothes in: you don't actually need much more than that. Here are some ways to have nursery staples do double duty:

- An upcycled dresser can also act as a changing table by adding a pad to the top.
- A diaper caddy is not a necessity. Chances are, you already have a basket or bin somewhere in your house that could store diapers.
- A glider is not a necessity either. Perhaps you already have a high-backed chair or rocker in your living room that could be moved to the nursery.

- Don't worry about toy boxes, bookshelves, or storage bins yet. Wait to see what you have and what your child will play with in a year before investing in these items.

You Don't Need Everything Now

A wait-and-see approach is a great way to implement minimalism in the nursery. Get a crib and then see how it goes:

- Perhaps you have a great crib sleeper who spends a lot of time in the nursery. You decide you want to do up the room beautifully because you're in that space a lot.
- Or maybe baby is not a big fan of the crib and is sleeping instead in the co-sleeper in your room most nights. You spend most of his waking hours downstairs with him on a blanket playing with a small basket of toys in your living room. You see that right now, a nursery upstairs, out of sight and earshot, wouldn't get used much. You prefer your son close-by so you can mix playtime with folding laundry, prepping dinner, or getting a few work e-mails in.

As you can see, it's tough to know how your days and nights will play out until the baby is born. That's why some minimalist parents skip decorating a nursery and wait until the baby is older to furnish and decorate a room for them instead. A newborn can't really tell you they like owls over trains, but your toddler or preschooler certainly could. Cribs have a relatively short usage span, but a twin bed could be used from age two onward—it could even be packed up and taken off to college! If you can resist your nursery-decorating urge for a few years, you can instead invest in furniture that your family can use for decades.

I Can't Stop Thinking about the Nursery!

Want to fight the urge to set up an amazing nursery? Here's how:

- Avoid looking at websites like Pinterest at *www .pinterest.com* or Instagram at *www.instagram.com* for nursery inspiration.
- Skip the articles about nursery décor in parenting or baby magazines.
- Focus on other aspects of a new baby, like a fit pregnancy, pregnancy nutrition, working on your relationship with your partner, and savoring your last months without a baby.
- Read fun fiction books, go out with friends, sleep in as late as you like, make complicated recipes and host a dinner party, or take a nonbaby, nonpregnancy, nonparenting-focused course, like beginner's French or memoir writing, to commemorate and enjoy these last few months of freedom.

Shift your focus to activities instead of nursery planning, and it will pay you back in more than cash savings.

How to Get What You Don't Have in Your Own Home

When you embrace a minimalist approach to housing, it may mean compromising on some *nice to haves*. For example, you probably won't own your own pool, two acres of land, or every children's book ever published.

It's Okay Not to Have Everything

Many new parents assume they *should* give their kids a large backyard, pool, and big playroom. But backyards and crammed playrooms are not a necessity for a wonderful child-hood. Most people overvalue having a lot of outdoor space and overestimate how much time will be spent in that outdoor space. For example, if you have a four-person family with two working parents, a thirty-minute commute each way, daycare and school drop-offs, weekend activities, and a harsh winter, you may only get good use out of your backyard on summer weekends. Tack on several hours a week in yard maintenance and it can be simpler and much more cost- and time-effective to make use of local parks and beaches instead of maintaining and paying for a large backyard year round. In fact, some stud-ies show that children in urban areas walk more and thus get more exercise than children who live in suburban areas. City kids, and their parents, travel on foot more and by car less.

So don't feel guilty; remind yourself that bigger does not mean better. There is an old myth that *providing* for your family is measured in stuff: a house with a pool, a big car, vacations to Disneyland, or extravagant birthday gifts. What if providing for your family was best measured by time spent with them and attention given and perhaps even, and this is a radical thought, giving yourself regular breaks from parenting and taking care of yourself, so that you can be present and engaged when you are with your family? What if you thought of providing for your family as caring for yourself and your children in the deepest sense? Instead of measuring in bedrooms or feet of granite-topped kitchen counters, what if you measured in hours on the couch reading books together or time outside or dinners spent together?

When you think that way, you can reject that society-led guilt and simply find ways to replace things you don't have. After all, they are much less important than the single thing you can't buy elsewhere—your time together as a family. This section will teach you easy, inexpensive ways to rent, borrow, or share items that you don't have in your home.

Participate in the Sharing Economy

The sharing economy is the concept of using community-based online services to share goods and services. The *sharing economy* has opened new doors to owning just what we need when we need it. Why pay to maintain, insure, and gas up a car that's parked in your garage four days out of the week? Why buy when you can rent or borrow? You can now rent an evening gown for one night, a Lamborghini just for a day, and even borrow a dog for an afternoon. You can rent a car by the minute or for the weekend with a few taps on your smartphone. You can even borrow power tools and ladders from tool libraries instead of owning a garage full of equipment that you will use for just hours each year.

When you become a parent, you can use this sharing economy in a whole new way.

- Children can borrow, instead of buy, new toys from toy libraries, refreshing their toy box and saving their parents money and space. Visit the USA Toy Library Association (USATLA) at *www.usatla.org* for more information and locations near you.
- Rent out your car when you're not using it. If you drive infrequently or have a second vehicle that sits in the driveway most of the time, rent it out for the day, or week, on Turo at *www.turo.com.*
- Have a garage full of tools that haven't been used since your DYI bathroom fail? Make some cash renting them out with 1,000 Tools at 1000tools.com.
- Use thredUP at *www.thredup.com* to find great quality secondhand clothing and sell your own unwanted clothing. This can be a great space saving and financially rewarding strategy for keeping closets trimmed.
- Rent toys instead of owning them. The company Pley at *www.pley.com* rents out toys for children of all ages. This is a great option for baby and toddler toys that have a short window of use, like shape sorters and beautiful and expensive wooden stacking toys.
- Use Airbnb at airbnb.com to rent out your home while on vacation or find baby-friendly accommodations

when traveling. This service is ideal for families: no need to pack the highchair or stroller or travel crib for that big trip when your home away from home already has the gear. And while you're exploring new sites, another family will be staying at your home and you'll be earning money from it. Looking for a no-cash trading option? Look for a house swap and trade a week in your home for a week in San Diego or Scotland.

- Join a hyperlocal parents' Facebook group at *www.facebook.com*. Search out a group that encompasses your immediate area and has just a few hundred members. These groups are an online village giving tips and news for families in a small area— think updates on broken playground equipment or reminders of an upcoming family event—and they are also a great place to find and loan out baby gear and household items. Borrow that bounce house for the birthday party from a family up the street, or loan your deluxe travel crib to another family a few blocks over. These local groups are often closed and you have to be added by an administrator, but a little hoop jumping is worth it for easy and feel-good sharing with neighbors.

Ownership is no longer a barrier to enjoying conveniences and luxuries big and small. Selling, swapping, and renting from peers is a great way to save money and live with less clutter.

Use Local Resources

While it's nice to have, say, your own pool, the cost of such extras is sky-high. Instead, look to local options where you can enjoy the fun of a pool without the time, money, or space needed to own one. You should be able to find these options nearly anywhere you live:

- **Libraries:** Kids' preferences change all the time. Buy a few classics and borrow the rest from your library where you can indulge the train phase, the princess phase, and the space phase without buying books at full price for each whim.
- **Pools and spray parks:** Save your water bill and meet friends at local water parks. Many are free or low-cost and offer sun protection.
- **Swing sets and playgrounds:** If you don't have the space or money for a playground structure in your own yard, fear not. Playgrounds are everywhere, and school- and city-owned spots likely offer more exciting options than you would ever put in your yard anyway. Look on local parenting group forums for the best options.
- **Bike paths:** If you live in an urban location, or a crowded neighborhood, it might be tough to go for a bike or stroller ride without dodging foot traffic. Look for local bike or walking trails you can enjoy free—saving the cost of living in an expensive suburban neighborhood.

- **Grills and picnic tables:** Many local parks have picnic tables and grills for rental. If your yard is small and you don't grill often, don't buy one. Instead, occasionally rent a grill and a table on a weekend afternoon. Cook, let the kids play in the park, and skip the cost and hassle of buying, storing, and maintaining a grill.

In addition to saving time, money, and space on these items, you'll also get the added benefit of meeting people in your neighborhood and community.

Housing Choices for Three Families

Living simply can be different for everyone. There's no one *right* way—just figure out what works best for your family. In the chapter called What Is Minimalist Parenting?, you met three different types of minimalist families—Beginner, Intermediate, and All-In. In the following section, you'll see how each type of minimalist family handled their living situation:

Beginner

The Beginner family is still in love with their small fixer-upper starter home. The original plan was to buy something bigger in a better neighborhood before the kids went to school. But that changed a few years in when they saw that the neighborhood was thriving and they were all happy there. Why change a good thing *and* take on more debt? Their lovely nursery furniture, a gift from family, lasted through two children before they donated everything but the convertible crib to a cousin. They embraced minimalism and stayed put. Instead of increasing their cost of living, it has stayed relatively the same all these years. Sure, things changed: daycare fees were replaced by a bigger grocery bill, hockey gear, and the costs of out-of-town tournaments. They've been able to live well despite their outdated kitchen, and the kids share a room when guests come to stay. Living below their means and being able to save for the future has been a great reward. They're thankful they avoided the stress of a more expensive home and the cash and time it would have eaten up. Besides, now that the kids are older, they can mow the lawn as a household chore!

Intermediate

The Intermediate family is going to stay in their spacious two-bedroom and den condominium until the kids leave the nest. The smaller mortgage means one parent can work in the nonprofit sector in a job he truly loves (which also has flexible hours so he can pick up the kids after school!). Having a smaller home to maintain means their weekends are free for whatever they really want to do: taking family trips to the beach, meeting up with friends at the neighborhood playground, etc. As everyone around them is sweating high car payments and furniture loans they took when they moved into five-bedroom houses, the Intermediate family is enjoying that extra wiggle room in their budget for date nights and saving up for a family surf vacation to

Costa Rica. Every day they're thankful that they made the decision to stay where they are and not upsize their home.

All-In

The All-In family is going to make a one-bedroom apartment work. They plan to spend just 15 percent of their take-home pay on rent as they stockpile cash to buy a piece of land. Once they buy the land, they'll spend weekends camping on the plot as they build their small home themselves and put up fencing for the live animals they will raise. At their apartment, they gave the bedroom over to the kids and have a foldout sofa bed for the parents. The lightweight dining table and folding chairs can collapse and be tucked under the sofa to create an extra play space for the kids or room for an inflatable mattress for an overnight guest. Taking a few extra steps to use their space for different activities has been worth it for the financial savings of less rent and the timesaving of a small home that's easy to clean and provides a short commute to work. The All-Ins will be in their self-sufficient, mortgage-free tiny homestead before the kids hit high school. Goodbye desk job, hello raising pigs, planting vegetables, and canning for the winter. That 600-square-foot apartment made it all possible.

Ten Things to Do Before the Baby Arrives to Make Your Home Run Smoothly

- Stock up on household sundries like toilet paper, laundry detergent, and dishwashing soap.
- Get current prescriptions filled.
- Change the oil in your car.
- Take your animals to the vet for checkups.
- Call in sick and take a day to hang out and do almost nothing.
- Clean out your refrigerator and freezer.
- Empty your junk drawer.
- Make some freezer meals to eat after the baby arrives.
- Set aside a postpartum wardrobe of stretchy clothing and early pregnancy maternity wear.
- Commit to no big changes for the next year—no moving, no renovating, no starting a new business, or starting an evening graduate school program. Make space to enjoy this one big change coming your way.

Gear & Clothing

You have succeeded in life when all you
really want is only what you really need.

—Vernon Howard

Researching baby gear can be a part-time job, as you spend hours test-driving strollers and researching what gear is best for your home, lifestyle, and budget.

Too much choice can be a bad thing, though. Overwhelm yourself with possibilities and you may struggle to choose which option is right for you. You'll look at twenty models, all with several pros and cons, with some in and just above your price range. What should be a fun and momentous event can quickly turn into a stressful process of trying to find the one single stroller that you and your partner love and meets all of your potential needs.

It's not even over after you purchase the stroller, either. Once you buy the stroller and start using it, you may think back to all the other options and wonder if you bought the wrong one. If you're someone who tends to over research a purchase, and often suffers from buyer's remorse, do something radical: give yourself less choice.

The Minimalist Way to Find Baby Gear

All of this choice often paralyzes us. We spend an exhaustive amount of energy comparing items and finally make a decision and we are less happy than we would have been if we had made a quick decision out of the top three choices. Less choice can be a good thing. Go minimal instead: test three items that suit your lifestyle and budget; pick one and be done. Once you've identified your needs (we'll talk more about that later in this chapter), look for just three items that are in your price range. It can be helpful to ask parents of toddlers or preschool-age kids with similar needs—live in the same style of home and have similar activities to you—what stroller they use and what they would get if they knew then what they know now. Make your list and then test-drive all three and pick the one that best suits your lifestyle. Do not get talked into something out of your budget. Turn a blind eye to that gorgeous baby bouncer that costs more than you spent on your couch and enjoy being done with one of the many small tasks for getting ready for the baby's arrival.

Or, if you want a bouncer and a friend loans you hers, accept it and move on. Do not compare that model to twelve other models and then convince yourself that you really should hunt down a different secondhand bouncer. You may be happier and less stressed in the long term if you just accept a secondhand item from a friend rather than spending hours comparing different brands and features.

When you're expecting a new baby, the nesting instinct can go into overdrive. You want all the baby things: every last piece of it. While you're going into the unknown of parenthood, checking things off a list, setting up swings and bouncers, researching and buying the best baby carrier, or hunting down secondhand steals on play yards, feels like preparation for the baby. It can actually be calming to buy things in the face of the unknown. But you could bring a baby home with little more than diapers and a few sleepers on hand and survive, even thrive. Stuff does not prepare you for the life-changing experience of adding a person to your family.

The stuff can clutter your living room and nursery and cost hundreds or even thousands of dollars that could be put to better use. The stuff can never replace a parent's voice and arms. Sure, some of these items could bring some welcome sleep or entertainment, but there is no guarantee that they will. Make a baby gear plan based on your budget, the size of your home, and your plans for growing your family and ignore all those must-have registry checklists.

What's Your Lifestyle and Budget?

The family in the suburbs has different needs than the family in the city who lives in a three-story walk-up with no elevator. The family who wants to buy high-quality, durable items second-hand that they hope to resell after using for just one child has a different need than the family who wants to buy new items at a moderate price, use them for two children, and then donate or give them away.

As you think about your unique needs and lifestyle, try to disregard all those must-have baby lists. Some people don't need a full-size stroller or a crib that converts into a single bed. Some families may invest in several expensive items because they hope to have a large family and will get many years of use out of the items. Other families may get by with very little, knowing that they are likely only having one child and would prefer to save money to hire a cleaner for their first year as parents, start a college fund, take a vacation, or offset the first year of daycare costs. Think about what will make things easiest for you when deciding on a strategy, budget, and types of baby gear.

Before buying anything, ask yourself these questions:

- What do we have storage and space for?
- How many babies do we hope will use these items?
- What is my budget? What do I want to buy new, and what can I live with being secondhand?
- Do I have any friends or family members who might be getting rid of gently used baby gear soon?

- What will our lifestyle be like with a baby? Will we drive most places or walk? Will we eat out a lot? Will we attend a lot of fancy events the baby needs clothes for?

The answers to these questions point you toward the gear that your family will use most often. Put your effort into those purchases and deprioritize other gear.

Clothing

What do people love to buy for new babies? Clothes. Whether you register for clothes or not, you'll likely get inundated with cute little outfits as gifts. (The other two most received gifts are baby blankets and stuffed animals.) People cannot resist sweet little sleepers, tiny fancy dresses, and micro-size sneakers (even though they are purely for show, as no six-week-old baby will ever actually walk in them).

Resist buying any baby clothing until a few weeks before the baby arrives. You'll probably receive a lot of clothing as gifts, so wait patiently to see how much you accumulate and then take stock and go out and buy the pieces you really need for the first six months. That's right; just worry about clothing for the first six months only. If you receive a lot of clothing in larger sizes, try to return them for store credit. You can then use the store credit as needed as you see what size your baby is, how quickly it is growing, and what items are needed for your local weather.

What and How Much Do You Need?

First, consider how often you do laundry. If you're in the habit of doing laundry once a week, you'll need more clothing than someone who puts a load in every other day. Think about the math on this: a baby under six months of age could need an outfit change three times a day. (Babies are messy in the early months. Exploding diapers and spit up cause multiple outfit changes a day.) If you do laundry every three days, that would mean having ten to twelve outfits to be on the safe side. If you're doing laundry once a week, you will want twenty-four outfits. If you don't have in-home or in-building laundry, you'll want to factor that in to how many outfits you have.

Second, think about what the weather will be like in your baby's first three months. A summer baby will usually be fine with short sleeve onesies, soft pants, and some lightweight-footed sleepers. A winter baby may need short sleeve onesies as an extra layer under heavier-weight footed pajamas or long sleeve onesies with a warm soft pant and socks.

Third, think about how big your baby will be at birth and at six months. Don't worry, that's a trick question. You don't know how big your baby will be at birth and at six months. That's why it's good not to stock up on seasonal baby clothing. You could have a baby who is twenty pounds and in one-year-size clothing when she is six months and it's winter, not summer like you thought it would be when you bought those adorable summer outfits for one-year-olds. Your baby may still be in six-month-size clothing as he approaches his first birthday. A great way to reduce some stress around parenting is to remind yourself that you cannot see the future. You're not managing a clothing store; you're just trying to keep your baby dressed appropriately.

Buy Mostly Used Infant Clothing

Infant clothing is a great thing to receive as a hand-me-down from friends, or to buy used, because many babies only wear something a handful of times before they outgrow it. The *used* item you find might look brand new or may even still have tags on it! So if someone asks if you want hand-me-downs, give an enthusiastic yes. If you're the first in your circle to have a baby, look on your local buy and sell website for anyone selling a lot of baby clothing, or check out a kids' clothing consignment sale at a local school or church. For the price of a few new onesies at the Gap, you could get a bag full of clothing that will last you the first six months. (Cleaning tip: if any of the hand-me-downs are stained, try washing and then hanging the clothes in the sunshine to dry. You might find the sun has bleached the stain out!)

Tip

Remember: clothing in the under six-month set is not an investment. Young babies are hard on clothing; they are most comfortable in very basic soft items and they love to wear pajamas. Buy secondhand, take hand-me-downs, and just have a little more than one laundry cycle's worth of clothing in each size. It will make your life, your laundry, and your closets so much simpler and saner.

Look for Comfortable, Easy Outfits

Newborns are small and squirmy and don't like having their cozy pajamas taken off. Complicated dresses with puffy sleeves and tiny jeans with buttons are a pain to put on, just to have to take them off an hour later during a messy diaper change. Those miniature adult-looking outfits are really cute, but they are far from functional or easy when you have a small baby. Would you rather spend time negotiating a tiny arm into a stiff pleather jacket or listening to your baby coo as you relax on the couch in comfortable clothes? Choosing the minimalist parenting method leads to those happy, stress-free times.

Buy simple and uncomplicated clothing for the first six months. Sure, have a special outfit or two for special occasions, for family photos, or to put a smile on your face after a particularly tough night. But make sure most of your baby clothing is soft and easy to put on and off. Choose elastic waistbands; zippered pajamas over snaps; and soft knits over denim, taffeta, or corduroy. Honestly, babies can wear sleeping attire for the first six months and no one will bat an eye.

A Simple Guide to Baby Clothing for the First Six Months

Most babies born in the six- to nine-pound range will wear newborn-size clothing for the first couple of weeks and will then move to a zero to three-month or three-month size (depending on the brand). Unless you know your baby is arriving early and will be on the smaller side, have just a handful of newborn-size clothing on hand. Nine-pound babies may only wear newborn clothing for the first week, so you don't want to invest in a huge clothing wardrobe that will barely be worn. If you need more clothing for a newborn, you can do a quick run to the store, see if anyone is selling used newborn clothing locally, or, the best option, borrow from a friend.

Tip

Forget the mittens that are supposed to stop babies from scratching themselves—they tend to be poorly constructed, fall off easily, and only fit for the first few weeks. Use ribbed newborn-size socks instead. They have a second use as actual socks, the ribbing keeps them snugly on tiny hands, and they fit a growing newborn's hand for long time.

Warm-Weather Baby Clothing

This is three to four days' worth of clothing. Double this amount if you know you won't do laundry more than once a week.

Newborn Size
- three short sleeve onesies
- three lightweight pajamas or footed sleepers
- two hats
- three newborn-size pairs of socks that can also be used as scratch mitts

Zero to Three-Month Size
- eight short sleeve onesies
- six soft knit pants or shorts
- six lightweight sleepers

- three pairs of socks
- two hats
- one fun outfit, such as a dress, romper, or polo onesie

Three- to Six-Month Size
- eight short sleeve onesies
- six soft knit pants or shorts
- six lightweight sleepers
- six pairs of socks
- two fun outfits, such as a dress, romper, or polo onesie

Cold-Weather Baby Clothing

This is three to four days' worth of clothing. Double this amount if you only do laundry once a week.

Newborn Size
- three short sleeve onesies for layering
- three long sleeve onesies
- two pairs of warm soft knit pants
- three winter-weight pajamas or footed sleepers
- two hats
- three pairs of socks
- warm booties

Zero to Three-Month Size
- eight short sleeve onesies for layering
- six long sleeve onesies
- six warm soft knit pants
- six lightweight sleepers

- six pairs of socks that can also be used as scratch mitts
- two hats
- warm booties
- one dress-up outfit

Three- to Six-Month Size
- eight short sleeve onesies for layering
- six long sleeve onesies
- six warm soft knit pants
- six lightweight sleepers
- six pairs of socks
- warm booties
- two dress-up outfits

Sleep Sacks, Swaddles, Blankets, and Burp Cloths/Receiving Blankets

You might think of this next category as soft furnishings for a baby. Depending on the weather in your area, and what your baby sleeps in, you may skip most of these and just have a few linen burp clothes to use for spit up and as a lightweight blanket. Again, evaluate your lifestyle and climate for baby's first three months to plan for just what you need.

Burp Cloths/Receiving Blankets

Burp cloths, sometimes referred to as receiving blankets, are a workhorse for the new parent. As a minimalist parent, you always want to be on the lookout for gear that serves more than one purpose. And boy, these blankets do! They:

- Shield your own clothing from baby spit up
- Act as a barrier for a sweaty baby sleeping on you
- Wipe up messes
- Line the bottom of a bassinet when the sheet is in the wash
- Create some shade in the afternoon sun
- Roll up into a wedge for tired arms when feeding a baby
- Act as an on-the-go nursing cover
- Act as a liner to change your baby on when at a public diaper-changing table
- And so much more!

Six is usually enough to get you through three to four days of spit up, blowouts, and other spills. Flannel works great, ages well, and can be used as a quick blanket backup or playmat on the go. Muslin also ages well and is a bit cooler, so it might be preferable if you have a new baby in a hot climate.

Swaddles and Sleep Sacks

There are a number of sleep-related items that parents often rave about as being a must-have. Tales of *good sleepers* are often the impetus to buy these sleepwear items, as in *my son slept twelve hours once in this swaddle, so I bought four of them*. Be wary of sleep tales. They are often exaggerated and specific to that one legendary baby who started sleeping twelve hours a night at six weeks old. Those babies were likely born that way, and the expensive temperature-control sleep sack their parents used had nothing to do with it.

You'll likely want to try a few sleep options, as most parents do, because you never know what your baby will like best. Buy them secondhand and in size zero to three months. A sleep sack, essentially a wearable blanket, comes in different weights for warmer and cooler climates. Swaddles also come in multiple options, from the classic muslin swaddle that you fold and tuck around the baby to make them into a *baby burrito* to zippered and Velcro options that don't require any technique or skill to put on the baby.

These sleep aids could be of great use to you . . . or they could be a complete waste of money and space. The only way to find out is to try them. If your baby loves a particular sleep aid, find one or two more in their size, in case you have a middle-of-the-night mess that renders the first one dirty. You'll find lots of new in-package or barely used sleep sacks and swaddles on your local buy and sell forum or on eBay at *www.ebay.com*; many parents buy them in a sleep-deprived state and then find that the clothing didn't magically make their baby sleep twelve hours a night.

Baby Clothing Strategies for Three Families

Here's how our three different families simplified clothing their babies.

Beginner

Generous family and friends gifted this family a mix of new comfortable clothing and sweet infant dress-up outfits at their baby shower. They exchanged some of the repeats and less practical outfits at the store for receiving blankets, a warm winter bunting bag, and some plain onesies in different sizes for layering. They splurged on a dress for family photos and bought a lot of different sleep sacks and swaddles off their local buy and sell forum. Once the baby outgrew the items, they stored them because they wanted to have a two- to three-year gap between children and they had plenty of storage space.

Intermediate

This family scored a great batch of infant clothing off craigslist at *www.craigslist.org*. They scored countless sleepers, onesies, booties, pajamas, a few outfits, a dozen burp cloths, and two brand new swaddle sacks for just $50. Family and friends gifted them a mix of clothing right up to size 2T. After sorting all the gifts, they decided to return the bigger sizes, and some of the more impractical clothing, for store credit.

Their child never took to the swaddle sacks so they sold them on a local buy and sell forum. Once all the clothing was outgrown, they picked out some of their favorites to keep for a potential second child and then sold the rest on craigslist. The burp cloths were in rough shape, so they cut them up and used them as cleaning rags.

All-In

This family received many bags of preloved baby clothing from friends. They sorted through the items, kept enough in each size so they didn't have to do laundry for four days, and donated the rest. A few people gifted them sweet dress-up outfits for their baby that they used a few times before donating. Between hand-me-downs and gifts, they spent zero dollars on clothing for their baby! Their baby loved being swaddled in a simple flannel receiving blanket for the first eight weeks (they learned how to wrap a tight swaddle off of a YouTube video at *www.youtube.com*). Once their infant outgrew the first six months worth of clothing, they passed it all on to a neighbor who was expecting their first child.

Strollers

Buying a baby stroller today is reminiscent of shopping for a car. There are so many options: all-terrain, urban wheels, easy fold, add-ons for a growing family, compatible with car seats, and coffee cupholder options for parents. It's hard to figure out what the right stroller is for your lifestyle, home, and city with all those choices!

A Stroller Questionnaire to Point You in the Right Direction

A first step to finding the right stroller: list what you plan to do and where you plan to go in your baby's first year. The following is a helpful questionnaire for starting your stroller search. Make a checkmark next to the statements that are true, and then narrow your initial search to the top three strollers that meet each need.

- I will be mostly walking on city streets/the mall/suburban sidewalks/in the country.

- I want to run or jog with my stroller.

- I plan to have another child in the next three years.

- I need my stroller to easily collapse for storage in the car trunk/at home.

- I use public transit—bus, subway, train—and need a stroller that can easily move on and off a train/bus/subway car.

- I plan to travel by air a lot in the first year and need a stroller that I can easily gate check/travels well.

- I want my infant car seat to snap into my stroller.

- I want a stroller with great resale value as I plan to use it for just a few years.

- I would prefer to wear my baby in a sling or carrier most of the time and only need a stroller for occasional use.

- I want a car seat that can easily move from car, to home, to stroller, or between vehicles.

The answers to this questionnaire will help you make a plan before you go into a store to check out your options. If you don't have your true needs in mind, you'll convince yourself to buy a beautiful stroller that is totally impractical for your lifestyle and is not in your budget. Families who buy impractical but fun or pretty strollers usually need to buy another one at some point.

Stroller Types and Styles

Based on the information you gleaned from the stroller questionnaire, you can start to look at one or two categories of strollers.

Umbrella Stroller
This lightweight collapsible stroller is called an umbrella stroller because, you guessed it, it collapses as easily as an umbrella. There is a range to these strollers, from very

lightweight, almost flimsy/cheap, to a sturdy/more expensive version that you could add a ride on board for a toddler, and it has a significant basket for diaper bags and groceries. The most widely regarded brand for collapsible strollers is Maclaren.

Pros: They are lightweight, easy to travel with, and inexpensive.

Cons: Many do not support infant heads or lay flat, so they are not useable from birth. Depending on the model, they are not a smooth ride, you are not able to use a car seat with them, unable to move the seat to rear facing to see parent, unable to use a bassinet with them, and many models have no storage basket or have just a very small basket.

Stroller Frames

This model of stroller is a frame on wheels that holds an infant car seat. Some of the top brand names are Baby Trend's Snap-N-Go and Graco's SnugRider. There are double and single options of this stroller, and they usually have a small basket underneath.

Pros: Easy to use with a car seat. You don't have to disturb a sleeping baby by removing them from a car seat to transfer them to a stroller seat. They are inexpensive or can be borrowed from friends.

Cons: The wheels are usually small and plastic, so they are not great for long distances or rough terrain. The handle height is usually not adjustable, so it can be a challenge for tall parents. There is a limited window of use: as soon as the baby has grown out of the infant car seat, you can no longer use the stroller.

Travel Systems

Want to buy your car seat and stroller together? This is called a travel system and it gives you an infant car seat and a full-service stroller. It works from birth until your baby grows out of the stroller, usually at age three or four.

Pros: One-stop shopping for a car seat and stroller that grows with your baby. There are so many affordable options and an increasing number of styles from lightweight styles to more rugged jogging styles.

Cons: You commit to a stroller and a car seat in one package. The car seat might be the exact one that you want and the stroller may not be the exact style to meet your needs or vice versa. The strollers in these packages tend to have fewer accessories and options, such as the ability to add a second seat or ride on board for a growing family. More premium brands are adding travel systems to their offerings, essentially selling you a car seat that is compatible with their stroller, but they are expensive.

Jogging Stroller

A three-wheeled stroller built for running. There is now a wide range of three-wheeled strollers on the market, and while some have *jogging* or *jogger* in the name, they may not be built to run with. A true jogging stroller will have a fixed front wheel or have the ability to make the front wheel fixed. Jogging-style strollers have become increasingly popular as everyday strollers.

Pros: Three-wheeled strollers turn easily and are great for both tight city spaces and rough terrain. Jogging strollers with large air-filled tires lighten the load, making it easy to push larger babies and toddlers around town or up hills. A true jogging stroller is a great option for an active parent to continue an exercise program with their baby along for the ride. The lighter-weight and more compact three-wheeled stroller, like the City Select from Baby Jogger, collapses easily. It's ideal for parents with limited space, for storing in a car trunk quickly, and for travel.

Cons: Most three-wheeled strollers have a smaller basket than a traditional four-wheel system. The seat on a three-wheeled jogging stroller usually does not fit a baby until they are four to six months of age. An adapter is needed to add an infant car seat or, in some models, a separate bassinet must be purchased so the stroller can be used from birth. True jogging strollers, such as the BOB brand, are heavier, take up a lot of trunk space, and in some small cars, you need to remove the wheels to transport it. Most three-wheeled strollers do not allow for adding a second seat and often are not compatible for a ride on board for a growing family.

Premium Stroller

This term refers to a range of strollers that are usually four-wheeled; offer a seat that can rear face, forward face, and recline; often have a bassinet included, or available to buy as an accessory; offer accessories to attach a car seat; offer accessories to grow with your family, such as a toddler ride on board or the addition of a second seat; have larger baskets for storage; and are in the upper price bracket of strollers.

Pros: Premium strollers offer a very comfortable pushing experience for parents and deluxe seating experience for babies. The wheels are usually air-filled tires or foam filled, and they run smoothly and easily over most surfaces. Premium strollers are useable from birth and adapt to your growing baby. They offer lots of accessories, some included at purchase and others available to buy separately, such as child snack trays, parent cup holders, parent consoles to hold keys and wallets, ride on boards for toddlers, deluxe weather shields, rain covers, and cold weather footmuffs. They are stylish and versatile, and if well cared for, they have a long life and good resale value.

Cons: These are the most expensive strollers on the market and most do not come with accessories, increasing your cost. They are the largest strollers and can be harder to maneuver around stores and tight spaces because of their size. They often require multiple steps to dismantling or folding to put into a car. Premium strollers are some of the heaviest strollers next to true jogging strollers. Some of their mechanics are complicated and costly to repair.

No Stroller Does It All

You want to run with your stroller, fold it easily into a car, and be able to add a second seat for a second child. Or you also want it to be lightweight and you want a seat that is able to rear face so you can see your baby on long walks. Sorry, there is no stroller that meets all of these requirements.

This is one thing to come to terms with when selecting a stroller: if you have a lot of distinct needs, one stroller may not meet all of them. One solution is to use multiple strollers, either by owning two strollers or by selling one stroller to buy one that is more suitable for the next phase of life. For example:

- You may use a stroller frame for the first four months with your baby and then move to a three-wheeled jogging-style stroller.
- You might have a big premium stroller with all the bells and whistles that you use on long trips around the neighborhood and take to the local coffee shop. Your second stroller is an inexpensive and light-weight umbrella stroller that you keep in the trunk of your car.
- Perhaps you know you want to use a baby carrier for the first few months and not bother with a stroller until the baby is much bigger. You can then decide to get a jogging stroller with a big seat for the baby to use at six months.

Whatever you choose, make decisions based on your lifestyle and resist getting a stroller because your friends all have it or just because you love the design.

The Minimalist Guide to Finding Your Perfect Stroller

- **Use the 90 percent rule.** Think of what your life will be like 90 percent of the time when deciding on a stroller. Yes, you may have one trip with air travel planned but that one trip shouldn't override picking a stroller that works for most of your day-to-day plans. Instead, consider renting a stroller at your destination (you can rent many kinds of strollers in most big cities or at theme parks). Some malls even loan out simple strollers for free. If you need a specific stroller near your home for a one-off occasion (maybe you're taking a rare hike on a wooded path), ask to borrow a suitable option from a friend.
- **Babywear instead.** Babywearing, using a soft wrap or carrier to carry your baby on you, can simplify your stroller needs. If you babywear in the infant stage, you can skip buying a stroller car seat adaptor or expensive bassinet attachments. Babywearing a second child can help you avoid buying a double stroller: wear the infant until the older child is ready to stop using the stroller or is able to use a ride on board.

- **Buy a secondhand stroller.** It'll likely save you a lot of money. Beyond the usual visual and mechanical checks, look for the stroller's manufacturing code. Most strollers have a manufacture date listed near the serial number. If there is no manufacture date, do an online search of the serial number to find the manufacture date. Strollers are a bit like cars: even if they look to be in great shape, they could have a lot of miles or years on them that are not visible to the naked eye. For secondhand strollers that are five years old or older, you should thoroughly examine the frame and wheels for excessive wear, and you should do some research ahead of time to find out what replacement parts, like wheels or a seat liner, cost. The ambitious and frugal expectant parent could buy a beatup stroller for very little and turn it into a dream stroller with some repairs, heavy cleaning, and a few new parts bought from the manufacturer's website.

- **Think long term.** If your desire for a high-end stroller is decimating your budget and stressing you out, think what you could do with that money if you were a bit more frugal. Calculate what that money (with compound interest from savings) could look like when your baby is graduating from high school or for your own retirement.

- **Consider options to expand its use.** Again, consider your lifestyle and see if one stroller could do double duty for you. For example, some single strollers can be made into doubles by adding a ride on platform. Some strollers with trays might negate the need for a clip-on highchair you'd take to a café. A stroller that comes with a bassinet could provide baby's sleeping space for the first few months.

- **If it doesn't work for you, sell it.** Let's say you realize a few months in that you bought the wrong stroller and you really need something that can fold up to store in the front hall closet. Sell it and buy the right stroller secondhand. Doing more with less—a mantra of the minimalist parent—means letting go of things that aren't working for you.

- **Remember, it's just a stroller.** Will you really enjoy those walks twice as much if you buy a stroller that costs twice as much as your second-choice stroller? Unlikely. After the initial buzz from a luxury purchase, we tend to get as much pleasure and use from the $200 stroller as we do from the $1,000 stroller. The minimalist parent recognizes the short-lived excitement attached to a luxury purchase.

Since no one stroller does it all, to keep life simple, find a stroller that suits 90 percent of your life and borrow, rent, babywear, or just make do for the other occasions.

Baby Holders: Bouncers, Swings, and More

Babies don't truly need bouncers, highchairs, swings, and any other baby containment or soothing device you've been told is life changing.

Take a minute to wrap your head around that minimalist thought.

Your child, and you, could actually get by without any of those bouncy, music-playing, big, plastic, floor-space-eaters. Several generations ago, parents held their babies, let them crawl on the floor, or laid on a blanket on the floor in the living room. Not long ago, parents fed babies food while they sat in an adult's lap, or once the baby could sit unassisted, they sat and ate on their own. Yes, you could skip the highchair, wait until your child is sitting firmly upright by himself, and have him sit on the floor with a bowl of finger foods. They would learn to eat all on their own. No highchair, no special baby bowls, and no fancy baby food machine required. Sure, you would have a lot of mess on the floor, but babies learning to eat are always messy. The fanciest highchair will not alter the amount of cleaning required after a ten-month-old has had a feast of sweet potato and avocado. (Actually, the deluxe highchair often increases the amount of cleaning with its divided tray, cushiony seat, and hundreds of crevices for smashed food to wiggle into.)

Sure, a swing could be just the thing that helps your newborn drift off for a much needed, by you and her, two-hour power nap. A fun bouncer could keep your three-month-old giggling and entertained for the exact length of time you need to send a few work e-mails in the early evening. The lightweight collapsible travel crib could be worth its price many times over for afternoon naps at Grandma's while you get some much appreciated baby-free time with your spouse. Or your baby may hate the swing or the bouncer or prefer his crib to the portable crib. After one afternoon holding a screaming six-month-old for three hours, Grandma may decide babysitting is too much for her. The lesson: you won't know if your baby likes one of these items until they try it.

The most minimalist parent may still want some gear: a spot to keep the baby contained while you have a shower or cook a meal, or a baby carrier for some hands-free time to make yourself a sandwich, or to go on an outing without a stroller. There are options for every budget and desire. Remember to refer back to your lifestyle demands or family plans (such as a small home or investing in pieces that will last through multiple children) when making decisions.

Borrow Baby Holders Instead of Buying Them

Borrow, don't buy, nonessential baby gear like bouncers, swings, and the like. Visit friends who have items you want to try and see if your baby likes it. Try out some local parent and tot programs and see if your baby likes any of their gear.

When your arms ache and you're running on very little sleep and you're ready to lay down your credit card for anything that claims it will keep your baby happy or help it sleep—

stop. Put your wallet away and, instead, ask for help. Call a friend or family and ask them to come over for a few hours so you can have a shower and some quiet time on your own. Switch off with your partner for an evening and go for a walk or meet up with friends. Something you bought at a store is far less likely to give you rest than help from people who care about you and your baby.

Bouncers and Rockers

A bouncer can be a great spot for babies under six months old to nap or be entertained. Some bouncers vibrate to soothe the baby and require batteries and others follow a more minimalist design and bounce in response to the baby's movement. Nonmotorized rockers need to be started with a gentle push, or a big movement from the baby can get them moving.

Now, the *but*. Like most baby gear, they often come in bright colors that will clash with your living room décor. In addition, their usage window is very small. Many bouncers can't be used once a baby is sitting up unassisted, and some have a weight limit of only twenty pounds. Keep all of this in mind if you feel you really need one. Buy used or borrow whenever possible!

Here are some minimalist approaches to living without a bouncer/rocker:

- Place your immobile baby on the floor to play. The original place to put your baby was on a soft blanket on the ground. No battery required on this one and nothing to store for a second child.

- Let baby sit in the stroller inside the house. Bring the stroller inside and park it wherever needed. Push the stroller from the dining room to the kitchen to the living room as needed, and if your home is one all on one level, every room can have a *bouncer* in it.

- Have a parent be the rocker or bouncer. Yes, the old-fashioned way was to use your arms to give the baby some soothing motion. It's a great workout, too!

- Wait it out. Somewhere around six months, babies learn to sit up unassisted: if you can use one of the alternatives listed above until then, you're out of the rocker and bouncer stage clutter free!

Tip

You'll probably see other big activity items in baby stores, like Jumperoos, doorway jumpers (which fit in doorways and let your baby bounce up and down), and activity chairs (the Evenflo ExerSaucer is one popular brand). Again, these items take up a lot of space and are generally unnecessary. If you feel you really need one, look online for a gently used secondhand option and save yourself money!

Swings

Some parents swear by swings as the most magical baby sleep aide ever. Other parents shake their fists at these monstrous machines that do nothing but eat batteries and floor space and anger their newborn. If your baby won't sit in a bouncer, or lie in a bassinet or crib for more than twenty minutes, maybe she'd like the swing. Before you rush out and buy one, though, borrow a friend's or even try one out in a store. Make sure your baby is calm when you test a swing: if they're already worked up and screaming, you won't know if they are truly swing lovers. Baby loves the swing? Great. You should be able to use it up to six months to get some peace and sleep. Baby hates the swing? Great. Skip it. You don't have to have that massive thing sitting in your living room or store it for a second baby.

Most swings run on batteries, but a few will run on a wall charger. If your baby loves the swing, opt for a model with a wall charger. Also look for options, like auto shut off to save power and frames that collapse easily for storage.

> **Tip**
>
> If you notice your swing isn't as effective and doesn't swing as well as your baby grows, you are not imagining things. Most swing motors have the same output of power regardless of the amount of weight in the swing. So, a smaller baby means lots of swing and a bigger baby means slower swinging. If your baby is a fast weight gainer, your swing will become less effective earlier than if he or she were a smaller and slower gainer. More reasons to skip the swing entirely or borrow from a friend!

Here are some minimalist approaches to living without a swing:

- **Babywear.** Many parents find that wearing a baby in a carrier isn't just an alternative to using a stroller—it's an ideal way to calm the baby down. Put the baby on in your carrier and go for a walk, vacuum, bounce on a physioball, rock in a glider, or simply sway side to side.

- **Push baby around in the stroller inside the house.** If you notice your baby is soothed and falls asleep easily in the stroller, then bring the stroller inside, push it back and forth, and use it to wind baby down for a nap.

- **Use your crib/bassinet.** A rocking crib or a bassinet on a rocking stand can multitask as a sleeping place and spot to put the baby for some soothing *swing* time.

- **Opt for a less expensive and smaller bouncer.** A basic bouncer or rocker can be rocked back and forth with your foot—creating a swinging action—to soothe your baby.

Baby Carriers and Wraps

Some babies never want to be put down. This is normal. Those tiny beings have been curled up tightly in a dark, soothing spot for months. That's their happy place. It makes perfect sense that newborns want to be held tight where they can hear a heartbeat. It's a wonderful feeling to have a newborn snuggled on you . . . but after a few hours you want to do things, like make yourself a sandwich or actually move off the couch. This is where a baby carrier or wrap can be very helpful.

A baby wrap is a piece of material that you twist and tie around yourself to hold the baby to you. They range in price and material from very inexpensive to the cost of a premium stroller. *Wrapping* a baby as it is referred to is a learned skill, and the more expensive baby wraps allow for a dozen or more different wrapping styles to hold the baby on your front, back, or hip. Wraps made of inexpensive jersey material work well in the early months when a baby is less than fifteen pounds. The more expensive linen and woven wraps can be used from newborn to even toddler age. There's a wrap option for every budget and skill level. The most commonly available wrap to purchase in stores is a Moby Wrap, and it's made of jersey material.

Tip

The carriers and wraps stocked at conventional baby stores are just a fraction of what's out there. If you have a specialty baby store in your town, one that likely sells fair trade or organic goods and cloth diapers, they usually have a larger selection of wraps and carriers to try on in person. The other place to test out wraps and carriers before you buy them is a babywearing group. Search for anything local to you that has a lending library of carriers and wraps or has meetups where members try out each other's carriers. This can be a great resource for finding the right carrier for you and your baby, and, bonus, a babywearing group can also connect you when buying a secondhand carrier or wrap.

Baby carriers are structured and don't require any technique to put on. A baby carrier is constructed with a waistband that ties or buckles around the parent and shoulder straps that tie behind the parent's neck if worn with the baby in the front, or across the chest if the baby is worn on the back. Carriers are very easy to put on, which makes them appealing for moms and dads. Like baby wraps, there is a range of baby carriers in price, features, and size. Many baby carriers require an additional insert for use with a newborn. Dozens of companies make baby carriers, and you can purchase everything from basic black in color to carriers that are customized with fabric that you select. The BabyBjörn Baby Carrier and the Ergobaby Carrier are two brands that you can easily find in stores.

When it comes to baby gear, carriers and wraps are generally very minimalist-friendly because they:

- Are versatile—can be used indoors and out; some varieties can be used until the baby is a toddler.
- Don't take up a lot of space.
- Are relatively inexpensive.
- Can even be made on your own with quality fabric and an online pattern.
- Can help soothe a colicky baby.
- Are very durable. Unlike a lot of big plastic baby gear, the baby carrier rarely breaks, needs almost no maintenance other than spot cleaning, and it can easily be sold or passed on to another family for use.

Not every baby likes being in a carrier or wrap. While they are convenient for parents, some babies refuse them. The only way to find out if you and your baby love using a carrier or wrap is to try one out.

> **Tip**
>
> You can make your own no-sew baby wrap! You'll need five yards of material that is 95 percent cotton with 5 percent spandex or Lycra material. Fabric usually comes in a forty-two-inch width, and a wrap should be roughly twenty inches wide. Fold your piece of fabric in half width-wise and cut down the fold. You can gift the second homemade wrap to a friend.

Portable Cribs and Play Yards

What exactly is a portable crib? A heavy portable crib is used as a bed or contained play area for babies and toddlers. It folds when not in use. Graco's Pack 'n Play is one very popular option, and BabyBjörn makes another good choice. Some of these play yards include a bassinet attachment for newborns and additional accessories, such as a changing station and attached diaper caddy. While a portable crib is on most baby essentials lists, many families will never need one.

Reasons to have a portable crib:
- For use as a primary crib.
- For use as a bed while traveling, if you can't rent one where you go.

- For use as a safe, portable play area or containment area for mobile babies.

Reasons to skip the portable crib:
- You have a crib or other sleep area.
- You won't be traveling with your baby.
- If you do travel with your baby, you will rent or borrow a portable crib at your destination.
- Your home is babyproofed and/or you have a safe play area for your mobile baby.

> **Tip**
>
> Portable cribs are one of the easiest items to purchase secondhand or receive free from friends who have moved out of the baby years. Most models are heavy and space eaters so families are all too happy to have a friend take them off their hands. The value-priced models are abundant in the secondhand buy and sell listings. If you really think you need one, make it a goal not to buy it new so you can save some money.

A portable crib is one piece of baby gear that you should really think long and hard about before acquiring. After all:

- Many churches, libraries, and community centers have a portable crib available for families with young children.
- Most hotels and vacation rentals store them for guests, and most grandparents go and buy their

own portable cribs while daydreaming of grandbaby sleepovers.

- You likely have numerous friends with portable cribs they aren't using.

As with other baby gear items, wait until you actually need a portable crib before buying one. You may just sneak by with borrowing or using hotel and community center options instead of buying, lugging around, and storing your own. If you can save those dollars and that space for yourself, do it!

> **Tip**
>
> A co-sleeper is a great alternative to a portable crib. Co-sleepers attach to the parent's bed, so baby is in arm's reach for overnight feeds and care. Many co-sleepers turn into portable cribs for use as sleeping space. Babies usually grow out of co-sleepers by six months so they tend not to have a lot of wear on them, making them an ideal second-hand buy. And if you buy a co-sleeper and it doesn't work for you and your baby, you'll have an easy time selling it.

Feeding Equipment and Highchairs

Before you run out to buy or register for a highchair, remember this: babies don't eat solid food until at least four months. Most babies can't sit up in a highchair until six months. So unless you have a lot of storage space, hold off on things like highchairs or baby-friendly cups and plates until you're ready to introduce solids.

Breast Pumps

The first type of food you'll have to worry about is breast milk or formula. If you want to pump breast milk multiple times a day, you'll need a breast pump. If you're not sure how much you'll need to pump, wait until you see how your feeding routines shake out before committing to an option. Because breast pumps are medical equipment that deal with bodily fluids, you can't simply try someone else's first. But you can wait to gauge your baby's eating habits, your body's response to breastfeeding, and your work schedule before buying anything.

Here are the three most common types of breast pumps:

- **Double:** The most efficient way to frequently express milk is with a double electric breast pump. This model is ideal for women who want to pump milk while at work, women who need to pump frequently to increase breast milk supply, or women who want to exclusively pump breast milk.
- **Single:** If you just want to pump the occasional bottle of breast milk, buy a manual single electric pump, like the Medela Swing Breastpump.
- **Manual:** Manual pumps, specifically the Ameda Purely Yours manual pump, are a good option if you want to express milk occasionally. Each woman is different, and some women find they can't pump a lot of milk using a hand pump, while other women find they respond best to a hand pump. The Ameda Purely Yours manual pump is compact, inexpensive, and easy to clean.

The Federal Drug Administration classifies breast pumps as a personal use item that shouldn't be shared. There is a small chance that even cleaned pumps that have had tubing, membranes, and flanges replaced could still harbor breast milk from a previous user. So instead of looking for a secondhand pump, check your insurance to see if they cover all or some of the cost of a breast pump.

> ### Tip
> Nursing pillows can be a great back saver for feeding your baby by breast or by bottle. If you receive a secondhand nursing pillow that's looking a little threadbare, you can refresh it by buying or making a new cover. The super minimalist mom can skip the nursing pillow and just use a firm bed pillow to save money and space.

Bottles

There are dozens of different types of bottles on the market. If you're buying them from a well-known baby store, they likely have met many safety regulations. Here's how a minimalist parent handles bottles: buy the cheapest ones and be done. Yes, there are bottles designed to reduce colic or gassiness in babies, and there are bottles made of glass and some with *easy feed* and *ergonomic flow* or other features. But they all essentially do the same thing: put milk in your baby's mouth. Unless your baby has a feeding problem that you know about in advance, just purchase a simple set of bottles that are in your budget range and be done with it. Save your decision-making energy for other things, like when to go on maternity leave and what your first meal after the baby arrives will be.

How Many Bottles Should I Buy?

Most people buy way too many bottles, and then they find they have to store them. Instead, start small and only buy more if you truly can't wash them fast enough to keep up with your baby's eating schedule.

- **Bottle-fed baby:** Buy six bottles. Once you've established your bottle washing routine, you'll know if you need more.
- **Bottle and breastfeeding, or exclusively breastfeeding with occasional pumping:** Buy two bottles and see how the first weeks go before buying more.

Bottle Brushes, Drying Racks, Bottle Sterilizers, and Bottle Warmers

You can really apply minimalism to this one category. You'll see so many gadgets for bottle-feeding and cleaning, and so many of them are truly unnecessary. A good strategy for deciding if you need or even want some of these items is to think: what would I do if I didn't have a . . .

- **Bottle sterilizer:** You would sterilize bottles in a pot of boiling water.
- **Bottle warmer:** You would warm a bottle by running hot tap water over it.

- **Bottle brush:** You would wash out bottles with a thick towel.
- **Bottle drying rack:** You would dry those bottles in your regular dish-drying rack.

As you can see, the world is not ending if you don't have these items. If you get them all, you're cluttering up your kitchen counters and cabinets unnecessarily. Starting simply, without any of these gadgets, is the easiest way to find out if any of them are useful to you.

Baby Food Processors

Here's another spot where you can pare down the amount of baby gear in your house. Making foods for babies doesn't require any special equipment, and again, parents in previous generations made do just fine without specialized baby food processors. If you're really desperate to make your own purees, look around your kitchen for something you already own. For example, use a:

- Fork
- Basic stick blender
- Food processor
- Potato masher
- Blender
- Mortar and pestle

The mushy baby food phase is not that long, and buying an appliance that eats cabinet space is unnecessary.

Highchairs

Highchairs are a great secondhand buy. Most models are built to last for a long time and get only a few years of use before they are passed on. Consider a minimalist philosophy when it comes to highchairs: simple is always better. A simple design means fewer parts to break and less area to clean. If you live in a small space, skip a traditional stand-alone high-chair and get a booster seat that attaches to a chair or a travel highchair that clips on to a table. Both options save space and are portable, and both can be used with babies in a wide age range.

The Ikea Antilop Highchair with tray has great design and is cheap. It's made of just seven parts: seat, harness, tray, and four legs that attach and detach easily. It's lightweight, easy to clean, and you can remove the legs to take the whole thing to your in-laws for Thanksgiving dinner. If you'd like a versatile, long-lasting feeding chair, check out the Stokke Tripp Trapp chair, which goes from first feeding to toddler chair to a child's chair, and it can even be used by an adult. This one chair could be used for a decade by multiple members of your house-hold. Its beautiful minimalist design will compliment any dining room. The Tripp Trapp chair is designed for use right at the table. These splurge-worthy chairs move quickly on the sec-ondhand market, so if you want one, keep a close eye on your local buy and sell forum.

Baby Monitors

If you live in less than 1,200 square feet, you likely do not need a baby monitor. When that baby wakes up and needs you, you'll hear him. Remember, baby monitors are new inventions. Parents used to wake up to the baby's cries from down the hall. But if you live in a very large home and plan to have the baby on another floor, or both parents are very heavy sleepers, you probably want a monitor. The rest of us can usually get by without one. That seems like a radical statement, when the norm now is a Wi-Fi-enabled video monitor, but applying minimalism means thinking differently.

> **Tip**
>
> On the occasion that you're vacationing in a large home, or, say, at a resort and want to put the baby to bed in the back room while you sit on the veranda enjoying the sunset, borrow a monitor or look for a secondhand one online.

Another reason to skip the monitor: you become overly attuned to your baby's sleep noises. Lots of parents find that listening to every snuffle and sigh of their baby sleeping actually steals a lot of their much-needed sleep. Babies often shift around and fall back asleep on their own over the course of a night. If you rush in his room at every minor squeak on the monitor, you're disturbing your own sleep pattern and perhaps even your baby's developing self-sufficient sleeping habits. Talk with your pediatrician about sleep habits to see what's best for your baby.

If you do want to buy a monitor, look for well-regarded brands like VTech and Philips Avent. Nest makes a high-end Wi-Fi-enabled version.

How Three Families Managed Baby Gear

Beginner

This family was spoiled with many gifts of baby gear and nursery furniture at their baby shower. Generous grandparents purchased the entire nursery set, which should last through any other babies; plus, the crib converts into a twin bed. After their shower, they returned many of the big baby gear items, like the exersaucer, play yard, and bouncer for store credit. A friend loaned them those big items for the first year, and they were happy to return them as soon as they were no longer using them. Their baby loved the Moby Wrap, so they used some of their store credit to buy one. With their driving lifestyle mixed with a walkable surburban neighborhood, they decided to buy the Baby Jogger City Mini Stroller. It fit easily in their trunk, was fairly lightweight, and was comfortable to push around on sidewalks.

Intermediate

These design fiends splurged on several investment pieces: a Bugaboo Bee Stroller, a Stokke Tripp Trapp chair, and BabyBjörn BabySitter Bouncer. The upside financially: they bought all three pieces secondhand but in great condition. It was money saved, and the gear should last through a planned second child and still be in good enough condition to sell once they are done with it. They purchased a mini crib that fit in their room and used it for the first year before eventually moving it into their second bedroom when the baby was four months old. Their Ergobaby Carrier, a gift from friends, was the only place their baby would take naps from months three to six, so they found it to be an invaluable piece of gear. They bottle-fed from the beginning and had a tight system of just six bottles that they washed every night. They installed a few baby gates, anchored furniture to the wall, removed everything that was on low shelves, and moved a standing lamp to their storage closet to babyproof the living room so they could avoid buying activity chairs or play yards.

All-In

This family escaped the first year with very little baby gear. A friend loaned them a co-sleeping bed, which attached to their own bed. They used that for the first four months, and once the baby was mobile, they gave the co-sleeper back and borrowed a simple travel crib that they kept in their room. One big splurge was a double breast pump, but they found it very useful to continue breastfeeding once mom went back to work. They made a homemade baby sling and bought a secondhand Maclaren umbrella stroller when the baby was three months. They spent two weeks at a cabin when the baby was six months old and borrowed a BOB Revolution Stroller from a friend for the trip. For baby-feeding, they picked up the Ikea Antilop Highchair and fed the baby anything soft and easy to handle from their own meals. They didn't have a dishwasher, so every night dad had a cleaning process that involved a bottle brush, a big pot of boiling water for sterilizing, and their regular dish rack. When mom quit pumping, they stored the pump for baby number two. They skipped all the exersaucers, bouncers, and jumpers: they simply didn't have the space. Their home was very small, and it was easy to just give away or store anything breakable or with sharp corners. It was easy enough to leave the baby alone for a few minutes playing on the floor, or if more time was needed, they put her in the highchair. Their biggest expenses when adding a baby to the family was the breast pump and, later, daycare costs.

Cloth Diapers

If you're absolutely positively sure you won't cloth diaper, move on. However, if you are even slightly curious about modern cloth diapers, saving money, or both, read on.

Cloth Diapers Can Save Your Wallet and the Earth

Just one baby can be responsible for thousands of diapers in landfills. A newborn baby often has a diaper change every two hours: that's a dozen diapers a day! Think of how many garbage bags of disposable diapers you could prevent from being in the landfill with one simple choice. That choice could also have a nice financial reward to it. Depending on the cloth diapers you buy, and how many children use them, you could save yourself a few hundred dollars or more.

Minimalist Reasons for Cloth Diapering

Yes, cloth diapers can actually make your life simpler and less cluttered. Here's how:

- You'll never run out of diapers. No more late night runs to the store.
- Save space with just one drawer of cloth diapers instead of jumbo boxes of diapers stealing your precious closet space.
- Fewer loads of garbage to take out.
- Less baby clothing to launder because cloth diapers contain outfit-destroying newborn poos better than disposables.

The Cloth Diaper Secret No One Told You

Brace yourself. This is a game changer and something no one talks about when they talk about cloth diapering: you don't have to cloth diaper all the time.

Cloth diapering has a wide spectrum. You can choose what works for your lifestyle, kid, and the often-changing needs of your family. The following are some ideas for part-time cloth diapering:

- Use disposables until the baby is big enough to fit into a one-size diaper (this style usually fits from ten pounds to potty training). A few weeks, or perhaps two months, in disposable diapers costs less than buying a set of twenty-four high-end—pocket-style or all-in-one—newborn-size diapers.
- Use disposables overnight. This could be from day one or from when your baby starts sleeping longer stretches.
- Use disposable diapers at daycare/out of the house/ on vacation.

You're starting to get the idea, right? Make cloth diapering work for you. When things stop working, change them. Maybe at some point you will decide to start using disposables for daycare and cloth diapers on weekends. It's okay. The cloth diaper police will not come knocking on your door.

Cloth Diaper Systems Today

There are so many cloth diaper options for parents today. It's no longer safety pins with a flannel diaper and plastic pants. The options for cloth diapering today are almost endless.

To find out which one is right for you, think about your cloth diaper needs, goals, and your lifestyle: do you want to save money or time? Will your child be at daycare, and will the daycare cloth diaper for you? Is your spouse on board with cloth diapering, or is it all in your court? Do you want to cloth diaper from day one, or will you wait until your baby fits into a one-size diaper?

You can also rent cloth diapers to try out different styles. This is a great choice if you're feeling tentative about using cloth diapers or if you aren't sure which style will work best for you. Some cloth diaper retailers will even give you a credit toward purchasing diapers when you return your trial set.

Buying Your Cloth Diapers

A good start is to have twenty-four cloth diapers. This number allows for the early stage when babies go through a diaper every two hours or so, and it will let you put a dozen diapers in the wash and still have diapers for that day.

Tip

Many families have an A set and B set of diapers. They have some less expensive or older secondhand diapers that they keep a half dozen of to use when they get behind on laundry or go through more diapers than they expected. Inexpensive prefolds with covers are a great backup set of diapers to have in your cloth diaper stash.

How Much Money Can You Save Cloth Diapering?

For the best savings, buy an inexpensive cloth diaper system, like prefolds and covers. This is by far the cheapest cloth diapering system, and you could save hundreds of dollars in the first year. You could even recoup the cost of your cloth diapers in the first twelve weeks and save more than $100. The following is a comparison of cloth diapers vs. disposable diapers:

- Cost of newborn disposable diapers for the first twelve weeks: twenty-six cents each diaper, twelve diapers used a day for twelve weeks for a total of $262.08.
- Cost of Real Nappies Cloth Diapers Essentials Pack, Newborn Size, for babies up to twelve weeks is $59.99.

The minimalist parent can cloth diaper to save money, reduce environmental impact, or even just for the simplicity of throwing in a load of laundry when you're out of diapers instead of going to the store.

How the Three Families Cloth Diapered

Beginner

The Beginners used a cloth diaper service for the first twelve weeks. It was very convenient—the company dropped off clean diapers and picked up the soiled ones. They were happy to save a few hundred diapers from the landfill, but it didn't save them much money. Once both parents were back at work, they decided to switch to using disposables.

Intermediate

This family wanted a simple system that would save them time. They used disposable diapers for the first six weeks and then switched to a set of twenty-four pocket-style diapers. It worked well and the diapers were in good enough shape once their child started potty training that they could use them on a second baby. Their cloth diaper goals were to make it easy, save a bit of money, and put fewer diapers in a landfill.

All-In

This couple was sure they would cloth diaper from day one. They actually pulled out their sewing machine and made some diapers out of old towels and T-shirts. They used infant-size prefolds and covers for the first few weeks and then started using their homemade cloth diapers. Their goal was to help the environment and save money.

Car Seats

This is one piece of baby gear that you definitely need if baby will ever be in a car. The big question when researching infant car seats is if you will purchase a convertible car seat or an infant bucket seat.

- A convertible car seat will last from birth, usually a minimum of six pounds, through toddlerhood, and even preschool age. Some convertible models change into a booster seat for school-age children.

- An infant bucket car seat can easily be removed from the vehicle and carried by the handle, or it can be snapped into a stroller. The infant bucket seat allows you to move a sleeping baby out of the car and stay asleep, and it provides a space for the baby when you bring an infant to a restaurant, friend's house, or doctor's appointment. The downside to an infant bucket seat is they are grown out of quickly, and you'll then need to buy another car seat for your growing baby.

Tip

Car seats are expensive, so it's tempting to look for a secondhand deal. However, car seats have expiration dates (look for it near the manufacturer's stamp and serial number) and once a car seat has been in an accident, it should be recycled and replaced. Unless you can verify that a seat has never been in an accident, you shouldn't buy car seats secondhand. If your budget is tight, look for the most basic model and remember that all car seats conform to the same safety regulations regardless of the price.

When deciding between these two types of car seats, consider how much you will drive with the baby and where you will drive to regularly:

- If you don't drive frequently, a convertible car seat may be right for you.
- If you drive a lot and/or have multiple vehicles, the infant bucket car seat is usually the best choice. Infant car seats can be strapped in with the car's seat

belt, or you can purchase a base that you install in the car. If you have multiple vehicles, you can purchase a base for each vehicle and easily move the infant bucket seat between vehicles.

Baby Showers and Registries: Tips, Tricks, and Alternatives

Are you filled with glee and anticipation at the thought of a baby shower? Are you excited to be inundated with gifts and to be the center of attention for a long afternoon of games, cake, and presents? Are you anxious to register for many, many things and then stalk that registry to see which big-ticket items your friends and family have purchased? You're not alone.

A baby shower for your first child is a rite of passage for a lot of women. It is something to look forward to, and in some cases, it is when you receive a lot of stuff. You get so much stuff at a baby shower: onesies, sleepers, diapers, bouncers, swaddles, and perhaps even some big items, like a stroller or a crib. Then you receive other stuff, like scratchy knitted cardigans, that you know you will never use or adorable tiny grownup outfits that you think you will use but never do.

You might also feel a lot of stress and emotions tied to your baby shower. Will you get those expensive items you were really hoping for? Will you be feted as you dream of with surprises and a lot of beautiful handmade decorations? Will your friends and family go all out? That's a lot of expectation for one afternoon.

Here's an idea: maybe the baby shower can be less about the stuff and more about the people. Much like your wedding day, you likely won't remember the gifts you got, but you will remember who was there and how they made you feel. You will remember that feeling of being surrounded by so many people that love you and care about you. Part of embracing minimalism is separating *stuff* from love. Your family and friends can welcome that baby into the world with plenty of love—and much less stuff. Now that you've read about minimalist parenting, you know the myriad of benefits it will give you and your growing family. But it's not always simple to explain those decisions to others. Your family and friends might have certain expectations for a big shower and long gift registry that you are suddenly not fulfilling. If you encounter pushback, you can gently explain your choices if you like. What's most important is that you are making informed decisions about what's best for your family. Here are some alternatives to the traditional, gift-filled baby shower.

No Baby Shower

Some people simply decide not to have a baby shower. They don't want the hyper-focus on gifts or they're shy and prefer not to be the center of attention for a whole afternoon. Some people also feel that celebrating a baby before it's born is bad luck. No matter the reason, no baby shower is a valid option.

Mother Blessing

A Mother Blessing is a gathering of female friends to celebrate the mother-to-be, and the focus is on supporting her as she prepares for the birth and arrival of the baby. It's an intimate gathering where your close friends provide advice and encouragement for the big changes you are facing.

Welcome Shower

A Welcome Shower is a party held a few weeks after baby arrives. It's casual—usually the parents host it with help from family or friends, and it's usually set for just a few hours in the afternoon: drinks, snacks, and a chance for people to meet your new family member. Usually there's no gift registry, but people may bring by something small or drop a meal off.

Preloved Baby Shower

This is an environmentally friendly and thoughtful way to fete the expecting parents. The host asks guest to bring something secondhand, either their own or sourced, for the new parent. People bring their favorite outgrown outfits from their own children or source a secondhand item that either the parent wants or they found useful themselves. The focus is on being kinder to the earth and giving the new parent something with a rich history from someone close to her. Seeing a well-made garment pass through several families can be rewarding, fun, and sweet for everyone.

To make coordinating a secondhand baby shower easier, visit a website like the Encore Baby Registry at *www .encorebabyregistry.com*. The Encore Baby Registry is similar to a traditional registry: parents select items that they would like to receive from lists on the Encore Baby Registry website. But instead of guests buying new items, they source them secondhand and then mark them as purchased on the registry.

Charitable Baby Shower

Do you have everything you already need or the means to buy them yourself? A charitable baby shower can be reward- ing for the host and attendees in so many ways. Guests bring either a monetary donation or baby item donation for a charity chosen by the expecting parents. Many families will never have a baby shower and will struggle to pay for basics, like diapers, formula, or keeping their baby clothed. This type of shower can be a great start in developing a long and rewarding relation- ship with a charity in your community.

Freezer Meal Baby Shower

As the name implies, skip the burp cloths and bring on the frozen homemade enchiladas. This is a great way to stock your freezer, let your friends show off their talents, and prepare for the arrival of your baby. You'll be thanking your friends every evening when you skip the evening meal-preparation grind and pop a premade homemade casserole in the oven. Time and nutrition are some of the most needed gifts for new parents, but they rarely receive them. Tip: ask people to make some single-serving meals for when one parent is at home with the baby.

Another idea for a meals-based baby shower: skip the gifts and ask your host to invite baby shower guests to sign up to bring a meal once your baby arrives. There are several websites that coordinate the sign ups and scheduling of meal gifts, such as Meal Train at *www.mealtrain.com*.

Registering for Baby Items

If you decide to register for a baby shower, do it the minimalist way. What way is that? It's not putting lots of big-ticket items on your registry. It's not agonizing over which swaddles to put on your list.

A Minimalist's Guide to Registering Basics
- Only register for what you know you need based on your family's lifestyle.
- Use a store with a great return policy. You want to be able to return items easily for store credit if people go *off the list.*
- Register for gift cards. Then, you can purchase items later if, and when, you decide you need them.

Maybe your baby shower will keep you in diapers and formula for a year, or maybe it will pay for a much-needed double breast pump, or maybe, just maybe, you'll manage through the first year and be able to use that store credit to donate much-needed diapers to the local women's shelter.

What to Register For

Here are some basic baby gear and clothing lists to work from. Remember, every family and baby is different. Depending on the season your baby is born in, its size, how often you do laundry, and the size of your home, and you may want less or more than what is shown on these lists.

> **Tip**
>
> Though they mean well, many people buy things not listed on a registry, such as stuffed animals, baby blankets, and fun but highly impractical baby outfits. If you find yourself swimming in baby blankets that you can't return, and a lot of clothing you know won't get worn, donate it to a local women's shelter.

Minimalist Registry List

- Newborn-size clothing: three short sleeve onesies, three sleeper pajamas
- Zero to three-month-size clothing: six short sleeve onesies, six sleeper pajamas
- Six burp cloths
- Bunting/snowsuit/fleece suit in zero to three-month size (winter baby)
- Diapers in size newborn, one, and two
- Small baby blanket

- A crib, bassinet, or co-sleeper
- Car seat

Additional Items to Consider Adding to Your Registry
- Six bottles
- Baby monitor
- Breast pump
- Nursing pillow
- Baby carrier
- Bouncer or swing
- Stroller

Thinking Big Picture

It's a natural thing to want to stock up on stuff for the arrival of your baby. This is one area where you might find minimalism challenging. After all, humans are hardwired to nest while pregnant—to store food and get our homes in order for the big change coming. This hardwired response is a throwback to a time of scarcity. Yes, not so long ago you really did need to keep every scrap of wood and can tomatoes all summer long to get through the coming winter. But most of us live in a time and area of abundance. Things are easy to come by and historically cheap.

Furthermore, back when scarcity was a concern, parents were not debating the merits of a video monitor over an audio monitor. Parents were simply hoping there was enough food for the winter and that the mother and baby survived childbirth. So if you find yourself thinking that you need a lot of stuff, take a step back and get some perspective. Remind yourself of those pioneers in covered wagons who raised babies without the midcentury modern–style rocker or the sleep sack in three sizes.

The Three Families' Baby Shower Strategies

Beginner

This family registered at a traditional big-box baby store and had a large baby shower with extended family and friends. They thought about their needs and storage space. Because they have a large attic, they registered for some items they wouldn't need for a while, like a highchair, and for gift cards and basics, like diapers and wipes. After the baby shower, they sent thank-you notes and returned most of the extra clothes and off-registry items for store credit. Soon after the baby arrived, they saw that they did want a baby bathtub and went and picked one up with the store credit. And when the baby started rolling over, they went back and got a playmat with a mobile. It was a simple system and with some unexpected gifts and some getting by with what they had, they ended the first year with enough store credit to purchase a twin bed to use when the baby outgrew her crib.

Intermediate

They had a preloved baby shower and used Encore Baby Registry (*www.encorebabyregistry.com*) to request a small amount of gently used items. The shower was a great gathering of friends and family; it was a cherished afternoon. They didn't get everything they wanted, but they filled out their wish list with great secondhand finds from their local buy and sell website.

All-In

This family skipped the baby shower and had a meet-the-baby party instead a few weeks after the baby arrived. They asked that if people brought gifts for the baby, they be hand-made or secondhand. They received several bags of hand-me-downs, a few sweet outfits, and friends loaned them a few pieces of baby gear. The baby shower was really more of a party and no registry was needed or wanted.

Ten Ways to Simplify Baby Gear and Clothing

- Buy for your home and lifestyle. Don't get caught up in the current trends or in whatever the latest *must-have* items are. Get things specific to your true needs.
- Buy less. Babies really don't need a lot. Less to clutter up your home and less to clean are good things when you're adjusting to being a new parent.
- Buy when you need it. Have just what you need for the first three months on hand when baby arrives. Bigger pieces, clothes, and items for bigger babies can be sourced later.

- Go high on occasion. Some baby gear can last through several babies and still be sold for a good portion of the original price. Splurge when you can make a good case for it.
- Go low on occasion. Many parents are desperate to get rid of their baby gear and clothing. Take the free stuff and save your money.
- When it's no longer needed, pass it on or sell it. Store your favorite pieces only if you plan to have another baby in the next two to three years.
- Return unneeded gifts for store credit. You can always buy it again later if you truly feel you need it.
- Keep baby clothing soft and simple. Complicated outfits and scratchy fabrics should just be for special occasions.
- Try before you buy. Your baby may love or hate the swing; find that out before you've actually bought one.
- When you're really tired, don't look for a cure in the form of a new piece of baby gear. Babies will eventually sleep and so will their parents. Until then, you and your spouse are the best and most reliable pieces of baby gear money can't buy.

Time

Time has a wonderful way of
showing us what really matters.

—Margaret Peters

The biggest adjustment for new parents: your time and your schedule are no longer your own. You can no longer just say yes to a last-minute invitation to the movies or decide to spend a Sunday curled up in bed watching Netflix or reading a book. There is now a human that needs to be fed, changed, and have an adult on call for her twenty-four hours a day. You've gained a beautiful sweet baby, but you've lost your ability to throw caution to the wind and go out on a bender on a Tuesday night or stay up until 2 A.M. in the morning organizing your college photos. If you're entering parenthood after a luxurious decade or so of freedom—your own home, good income, and very little responsibility to anyone other than yourself—this can be a tough adjustment.

This new time crunch can cause tension between partners. One spouse may start keeping a mental or even written list of who got more sleep that week and how many times one spouse has had a personal night in the last month. When people feel that they aren't getting the amount of personal time they need, or that they aren't ready to commit to the new schedule, small slights of stolen time will appear. Arguments over whose turn it is to be up with the baby will have you both awake in the middle of the night.

Of course, babies aren't always challenging or disruptive. Sometimes newborns are very cooperative and will sleep right through that brunch with friends. Sometimes the at-home baby-watching parent has an easy gig because the baby sleeps the entire time, while the other parent is out at Bible study or hot yoga. Wins all around.

The Minimalist Approach to Time Management

The minimalist parent is often born in those first few months with a new baby when it's so obvious what is truly worth your time—nourishment, sleep, hugs, fresh air—and what isn't. This new sense of how finite time really is can make your priorities, the things that bring you joy and you hold dear, very clear. It's one of those silver linings to the sleep deprivation and losing a bit of spontaneity: those hours that you once took for granted are valuable and hold a little more sparkle. You'll never say you're bored again. A sunny winter afternoon walking to the grocery store is no longer just twenty minutes of time passing, but a moment to get some joy out of, to inhale the crisp air, to savor the sight of your baby bundled up and fast asleep in her stroller. The minimalist parent knows that time is their most precious commodity and they spend it wisely.

Minimalist time management starts by taking stock of all these new demands on your time—how it's spent now, how you wish it was spent, who's doing what—and determining how you can reconcile all these things in a way that works for your family. It also means challenging assumptions you might be carrying and re-evaluating expectations that you can do everything. One of the benefits of minimalist parenting is that you'll carve out more time for what's important to you—but first you'll need to prioritize, communicate, and ask for help when you need it. We'll walk through all the challenges of managing time with a baby in this chapter.

Decide to Do Less

You can adopt a minimalist approach to time even before the baby is born. Start easy: scale back your plans. If you can avoid or delay big life changes at the end of a pregnancy, or with a young baby, do so at all costs. The first months, really the first year, of parenthood is not a time to sell your home, tackle a large home renovation, or start an evening graduate degree program. Sometimes these events are out of your control, but try to take on as little as possible in this time frame. Instead, focus on the little things. Prepare for those first six weeks of parenthood as you would if you knew in advance that a blizzard was eminent. Prepare a lot of food, stock up on nonperishables, clean the house, make sure the laundry is all done, and get ready to hunker down at home for a few weeks.

If you wrote a long list of tasks and projects that you plan to get to on maternity leave, rip it up. A sensible maternity leave plan involves as much sleep as possible, light activities when able, meeting up with friends, maybe some parent and baby activities, and hopefully a freezer stocked with meals for the first six weeks. Maternity or paternity leave should not be a time to tear down walls, write exams, or plant an extensive vegetable garden. If you find that your baby is *easy* and you seem to have a few hours a day of genuine boredom, maybe, just maybe, finish a knitting project, get to some books on your must-read list, or decide to make something for dinner from scratch instead of defrosting one of the dozen lasagnas in your freezer. New baby time is a time to lay low, get your bearings, and survive. Saving the world or tiling your bathroom can wait.

Before Baby Arrives:
Divide Up the Household Chores

Here's a good task to complete with your partner before the baby arrives: make a list of all household and family tasks. Then decide who will be in charge of which task. Put everything on this list, from the day-to-day tasks, like:

- Unloading and loading of the dishwasher
- Cooking
- Cleaning
- Laundry
- Grocery shopping
- Sorting through the mail
- Taking out the trash
- Pet care

Add the infrequent things, like:

- Booking doctor's appointments
- Getting vehicles serviced
- Home maintenance and repair
- Yard maintenance

When a new baby arrives, the default *household chores* partner often becomes overwhelmed. If they were already doing 75 percent of household tasks before the baby arrives, they will struggle to keep up with those tasks once an infant is added to the family. It's better to get the other parent up to speed and sharing in the household workload before there's a baby at home to care for.

Once you have a detailed list of all of the tasks and household work, flag the ones that aren't essential to surviving or that you could outsource for a short time or do in advance (more on outsourcing later in this chapter). It could be as simple as restocking essentials, like toilet paper, a few weeks before your due date or hiring out yard maintenance for the first two months. As the saying goes, "babies don't keep." There will be time in the future, a time without babies to hold and rock to sleep, when you can eliminate the dust bunnies and keep up with your usual cleaning standards.

> ## Tip
> Cross-train so both parents can jump in on any household task. This is particularly important if you plan to exclusively breastfeed. Nursing a baby takes a lot of hours. You'll be sitting in a chair or on the couch feeding for long stretches and be unable to do your usual amount of housework. So while your partner may not be doing feedings, he can still fold the laundry, make a meal, and put away groceries.

After you remove the nonessential items from your list, begin breaking the list into who will do what. These assignments don't need to be set in stone for a lifetime—they're meant to set reasonable expectations of who's responsible for which chores in the near future. They should take into account working hours, but that doesn't mean that a stay-at-home parent should do everything. Duties should be shared, even by the working parent. If, at any point, the system isn't working well, go back to the drawing board, reassess the list, and reassign tasks in a way that makes all parties satisfied. This list will need to be updated and adjusted once or twice a year as parents change working hours, move to a home with a no upkeep yard, pick up new routines or systems (like batch cooking on weekends or start or quit cloth diapering), or the baby begins going to sleep later.

Completing Household Chores
Is Not Personal Time

Some days, it can feel like the parent cooking dinner has the fun job and the parent bouncing the cranky baby is doing the real work. It's true, taking a break from baby care and doing household chores can be a welcome change of pace on those days you spend two hours trying to get the baby to nap. But shoveling snow or repacking bulk meat to freeze are not personal time activities. If both parents are struggling with the full-time demands of parenting and the lack of free hours in their schedule, basic housework sometimes slips into the *time off* column. This is one of the reasons to really focus on making a list of household chores before the baby arrives. Both parents need to know and share the work of running a home and being a parent.

Even if life gets ahead of you and your bathroom sink is growing new strains of bacteria and the floors have only been cleaned by the dog licking them, fight the urge to use your *off baby duty* evening to clean the house. Return to your list of essential tasks; you can survive with somewhat clean clothing and the most basic of meals, but you will not survive without some downtime. Even if that downtime is thirty minutes in your bedroom eating some crackers and reading the Sunday paper, or painting your toe nails, that short time of not being in charge of a baby and not dealing with housework can be a restorative and much-needed break for a new parent. So let your standards slide for a few months. The refrigerator will get cleaned out and wiped down when you've strung together a week of good sleep.

Chores, Shopping, and Upkeep: Outsource As Much As You Can

Which would you prefer: a new postpartum wardrobe or not having to scrub a toilet or wash a kitchen floor or clean windows for an entire year? Or would you prefer the brand new luxury stroller, the one that you only use on weekends, over not arguing with your spouse each week about whose turn it is to clean the bathrooms? If time is your most scant resource and you have room in your budget, look into outsourcing household and personal tasks. Outsourcing can grease the wheels for parents who are strapped for time. It's also a way to bring the practice of minimalism into how you spend your time— stop doing the things you *specifically* don't need to be doing. It doesn't matter if you personally go to the store and buy baby food; all that matters is that the baby food is in the house when your baby is hungry.

If you have the means, hire out as much as you can:

- Grocery shopping
- Household goods shopping
- Yard maintenance
- Cooking/meal prep
- Dry cleaning drop-off/pickup
- Cleaning

- Taxes
- Walking the dog, even if for only one of the daily walks

Think of every outsourced hour of work as time you can:

- Spend with your baby or sleep
- Give to your spouse as personal time
- Use as precious personal time for yourself

Delivery Services

If you only choose one task to outsource, consider grocery/home goods deliveries. You need food and toilet paper, so you can't avoid these tasks—they have to get done. But they don't have to get done by you or your partner. There may be a small delivery fee, and yes, someone else will be picking your produce, but those are small prices for literally creating more time for yourself. In addition, staying out of the stores can eliminate all those little impulse buys that balloon the grocery budget. If you buy other products online, like diapers and cleaning products, set up automatic ordering based on usage so you have one less thing on your to-do list. You can save time *and* money by using those types of services. Just make sure you don't order more than you need or can store.

The range of things you use all the time and can schedule deliveries for is almost unlimited:

- Food
- Produce
- Diapers and wipes
- Paper goods: toilet paper, paper towels, napkins
- Toiletries
- Pet food and cat litter
- Cleaning products and dishwashing soap, laundry detergent, dishwasher detergent

If you are a contractor or work an hourly wage, you know exactly what your time is worth. It may be more beneficial to you and your family to work an extra two hours a week to pay for outsourcing the yardwork and housecleaning. Work a bit more during the week so you can triple the hours you spend relaxing with family on the weekends.

Outsourcing and Budgeting

If your budget doesn't currently have the room for out-sourcing, but you are desperate to have more free time, examine your budget for any nonessentials.

- If you always order pizza on Friday nights and go out for lunch at a restaurant every Sunday, could you make a frozen pizza instead and do the big lunch out every other week?
- Could you tweak your spending habits to find the money for that weekly lawn care and yard maintenance that eats up a lot of your weekend?

The dual-income family with a young baby can benefit greatly from outsourcing some tasks. If there is even a sliver of room in your spending—food waste, the once a month *fun* shop at Target—exploit that and pull back in some other areas so you can get more help.

Ask for Help

Minimalist parents ask for help when they need it because they know the value of gifting people their time and service. One of the greatest lies of modern parenthood is that you are supposed to do it all on your own. The baby, the job, the house, and finding some time for you can max out even the most organized and motivated individual. It really is supposed to be a village of grandparents, aunts, and uncles helping parents care for and raise children.

So if anyone is willing to help, let him or her help. If you think there is a chance someone will help, ask them. Maybe the grandparents can pick the baby up from daycare once a week and make dinner at your house for you. Maybe your uncle, who lives down the road and is retired, would be happy to shovel your driveway on snow days. Maybe some of your friends who don't have kids are waiting for you to ask them to watch the baby for a few hours on the weekends. Ask for help. Maybe your mother-in-law would be delighted to come to your house once a week and do her favorite thing—laundry. Asking for help from friends and family is not a sign of weakness, but rather a sign that you know your limits and trust the people around you.

The First Six Weeks: Survival Mode

Once baby is born, you're suddenly thrown into the thick of parenting. The first six weeks with a newborn are all about survival. Sleeping and eating are the two priorities for all involved parties. Do not worry about how much takeout you have eaten, or that you wore the same clothes three days in a row, and, actually, they were pajamas. Do not worry that this is what will happen for the rest of your life: it's not. It's a small window of *lovely, soft, tiny baby folded up on your chest for six hours a day* chaos.

Everyone wakes up a few weeks into having a baby and wonders: will I be stuck on this couch forever? Will I always brush my teeth for the first time each day after lunch, which I now eat at 4 P.M.? The answer is no. It will get better. It will get a bit more predictable—you'll figure a few things out, and the baby will figure a few things out. Soon you'll be high-fiving your spouse when you got the baby down to bed before 7 P.M. and then prepared a meal from scratch together.

Tip

Create a parent feeding and entertainment basket filled with snacks, a water bottle, a book or magazine, baby nail clippers, diapers and wipes, and a few burp cloths/receiving blankets. Have it at arm's length for when you get trapped under a sleeping baby, your phone battery is almost dead, and you need food and entertainment nearby.

How to Manage the Overnight Hours

One of the biggest mistakes new parents make is both of you staying up during a hard night with the baby. In the first few days, some of this may be inevitable and a very natural start: you want your partner there comforting both you and the baby as you change your first diaper explosion and have to give baby his first bath at home as the sun comes up. However, after the first week to ten days, it's important for everyone to start a shift system. The minimalist parent is always looking for efficiencies for fun, work, and, of course, sleep.

Both parents should be guaranteed some blocks of uninterrupted sleep when you have a newborn. Even if one parent is staying at home and the other is going to work in an office, both parents' sleep should be prioritized. Staying at home with a newborn is tough work and just as, or more, physically taxing than sitting at a desk for nine hours. Yes, the parent who needs to be in top form mentally or physically at work—say because they operate heavy machinery or they are presenting in court—should get priority for sleep. Even if someone needs to be rested for work, a plan ought to be in place so the other parent can catch up on sleep during the weekends. A solid family sleep plan includes sleep for everyone.

Consider a "Sleep Shift" Arrangement

Be prepared for some early nights in the first six weeks, or even up to the first three months. Here's one way the *shift* schedule could work:

1. Ideally, one parent takes the first shift of sleep, giving the last bottle or feeding in the early hours of the evening and then immediately going to bed for an uninterrupted four-hour window (earplugs and a sleep mask may be good investments).

2. The other parent is *on call* for that four-hour shift. They can sleep if they like, but they should take care of any needs the baby has in that four-hour window.

3. The next waking after the four-hour slot is the start of the second shift, and the parents trade spots.

Keep up the shift system until your baby starts having reliable chunks of three to four hours of sleep and goes back to sleep quickly after wake-ups.

This shift system is great for sleep and survival . . . but not always great for socializing or your relationship. Here are some ways to address those potential drawbacks:

●   One night a week, you both stay up for the first two hours together. Hopefully, the baby will sleep, but if not, you both tend to the baby in between Scrabble moves or by putting the movie on pause. Condense the rest of the night into two shifts.

●   On a Friday or Saturday night, you can reconnect and hopefully shift your routine to the next morning: the parent on first shift sleeps in while the second shift parent takes care of the baby. The parent on second shift gets a nap in the afternoon.

- Try to swing some couple time at home on a weekend afternoon while the baby is napping.

Keep Nighttime Interruptions . . . Minimal

You certainly can't control a whole lot in those first six weeks. But you can attempt to make the nighttime environment prime for sleeping. Here are some tips for minimizing disruptions overnight:

- **Try to only change dirty (read—poop!) diapers overnight.** Undressing a baby and changing their diaper will wake them up further.
- **If necessary, change the baby first.** If the baby is very awake during the night, change his diaper before you feed him. In the early weeks and months, most babies fall asleep at the end of a feed. Keep that baby asleep!
- **Keep the lighting dim.** If you're on first shift and have the baby in a bouncer while you watch television, dim the lights and face the baby away from the television light. If the baby is in a nursery, avoid turning on overhead lights: use a nightlight or a light from the hallway to assist you.
- **Keep noise to a minimum.** Turn on closed captioning on your television so you don't miss any jokes on your favorite sitcom. Ambient white noise and low-volume mechanical noise, like a dishwasher running or the

hum of an air conditioner, are just fine and may even
help the baby sleep.

- **Keep that handy parent feeding basket near you.**
  It's great to have all of your supplies close at hand
  for middle of the night burpings, changes, and even
  hydration for mom and dad. It's not just baby who
  should be kept sleepy at overnight wake-ups: mom
  and dad should try and keep themselves drowsy too.
  If you're bottle-feeding overnight, prep bottles in the
  early evening and keep them in a cooler bag, ready
  to go in the feeding basket.

- **Resist looking at screens.** Yes, flipping through Instagram on your phone or reading e-mails while rocking
  the baby can pass the time, but it will make it harder
  for you to fall back to sleep. Looking at lights from
  screens interrupts the circadian rhythm that tells your
  body when to sleep. Since you already have a newborn baby messing with your sleep, you don't need
  anything else stealing your slumber. So try to sit back
  and relax while rocking the baby to keep your brain
  drowsy. Limiting screens for overnight parenting will
  help you get yourself back to sleep faster, and it will
  make the limited sleep you do get more restful.

Limit Visitors in the First Six Weeks

The other minimalist parenting tip about enjoying the first
weeks with your baby: guard your privacy. The first days and
weeks after a baby is born are a wonderful but often frag-

ile and exhausting time. Hormones and lack of sleep can lead to a lot of tears. It can also lead to a very normal but strong desire to nest in your home with just your baby and partner. It is completely normal and okay to say no to visitors. Don't make firm commitments on visitors for the first few weeks. Let people know that swinging by to see the baby will be contingent on how everyone is feeling that day. Some families even designate a *babymoon* and ask family and friends not to visit for the first two to six weeks so the parents can rest and bond with the baby.

If people are visiting, make it clear that they shouldn't stay long, unless they are there to help. Help means unloading the dishwasher, doing laundry, or making a meal.

This is especially not a time to have people who are not actively helping you stay in your home. If family must stay with you, be clear that they will need to act as hosts and do their own meal preparation and tidying for the duration of their stay. Houseguests should be prepared to make themselves scarce for long segments of the day, to be silent overnight, and to leave your home in better condition than it was when they arrived.

Your New Schedule: Working Parents

Once your maternity/paternity leave has ended, it's time to face the reality of your new schedule. Yes, this can be a very emotionally trying time for everyone—you are probably experiencing dozens of feelings that change from one moment to the next: sadness, excitement, guilt, anticipation, relief, anxiety, and on and on and on. Despite all the changes and uncertainty, you can still find peace with this new life. And you can still approach it with a minimalist attitude.

Most families have both parents working outside the home today. This is the new normal. So let's embrace all the good things about dual-income families. Here are some reasons to look forward to going back to work after paternity or maternity leave:

- You get to go to the bathroom alone.
- Lunch. Delicious lunch that you can eat when you want and where you want. Plus, you can finish your coffee before it gets cold.
- Interaction and conversations with other adults that have nothing to do with the regularity or irregularity of your baby's bowel movements.
- Clothing that will not get spit up on it for a whole nine hours. *Unless you work in a daycare or as a nurse.
- Money!
- An opportunity to engage in challenging work that you pride yourself on, that provides an opportunity for you to learn new things, and that feeds your soul. (Hopefully, some of this about your job is true.)
- A break from parenting. There is no shame in saying you'd like forty hours a week off of baby duty. There are 168 hours in every week, so spending forty of

them without your baby, roughly 24 percent of your time, isn't really that much.

Whatever your reason for heading back to work, your best bet is to make a plan ahead of time. Build your new family schedule while you're pregnant and tweak it as your return to work approaches. Leave room for change and build in some trial runs. Do not wait until the day before you return to work to test if you really can be up at 5:30 A.M. to feed the baby, pump milk, shower, get changed, pack the daycare bag, pack your lunch, pack your gym attire, make yourself presentable for work, and be out the door by 6:15 A.M. every morning.

Daycare Prep

Let's assume your baby will be heading out to daycare while you and your partner work. That means some busy mornings getting everyone up, dressed, and fed before hitting the road at an early hour. You can't always change how much there is to do, but you can change how and when you get the tasks done. That's where minimalism comes in. The key to a smooth-running morning actually starts the night before. You'll reduce your stress, minimize the possibility of forgetting things, and start your day on the right foot if you do as much as you can the night before.

The best way to push yourself to do it the night before is to implement a rule that no one sits down in the evening until everything is done. If he's bathing the baby and doing other bedtime routines, you're cleaning up after dinner, throwing a load of laundry in the washer, and starting to prep the daycare bag and tomorrow's lunches. It may be tempting and almost reflexive after a long day of work and parenting to lounge around the kitchen snacking on chocolate-covered pretzels and playing *Candy Crush*. Fight this urge and finish the dishes while the other parent is completing the precise twenty-three-minute bedtime routine for your five-month-old. When bedtime is done, the other parent should be back in the kitchen helping you with daycare prep, lunches for work, and folding the load of laundry that just came out of the dryer. You can high-five each other as you fall on to the couch, or into bed, at 8 P.M.

How can you actually save time doing things the night before? Think of it this way: making a sandwich the night before takes two minutes, but it'll take ten in the morning when you're distracted and rushing. Instead of cursing traffic because you're running late and starting your day already on the verge of a breakdown, you'll enjoy a precious extra minute saying goodbye to your baby as you leave daycare. Those few minutes are the difference between rushing into work stressed out and five minutes late and arriving a minute early. That's where you'll see the timesaving effects of minimalism.

Repeat these mantras:

- Always do as much the night before as possible.
- No one sits down in the evening until everything is done.
- Everyone sleeps better when bags are packed and lunches are made the night before.

Do not let yourself, or your spouse, convince each other, "Oh, we will do that in the morning." You will end up doing it in the morning, but you'll both be late and resentful about it. Sure, you may have an eight-minute buffer built into your morning routine, but one *forgot that* error later and you're fifteen minutes behind schedule. Plus, babies sense when you've decided to let your routine slide a bit. That's when they do things, like spit up their morning bottle of milk all over themselves or have an explosive diaper just as you put the car seat in the car.

Sort Out Pickups and Drop-offs

For some families, there is only one choice for meeting work obligations and staying within daycare hours for childcare: one parent drops off and the other parent picks up. One parent starts work earlier and does evening pickup and the other parent drops off the baby at daycare and starts and finishes work a bit later. You'll set your schedule based on the flexibility of work schedules, commute times, and the hours of caregiving available.

Even if one parent has a more flexible work arrangement, resist the temptation to leave every daycare drop-off and pickup on that parent's schedule. Just because one parent can take work home with them and has a casual office schedule does not mean they actually have less work. Both parents should discuss with their employer how their schedule will change once the baby arrives. You may need to block out your online work calendar and not accept 5 P.M. meeting requests now that you need to leave work at 5:15 P.M. every night to pick up your daughter.

Sample Schedule for Two Working Parents

The following is a sample schedule for families with a thirty-minute commute for both parents, daycare located between work and home, and both parents working a nine-hour day.

6 A.M.: Parent A showers and gets ready for work.

6 A.M.: Parent B gets baby up, feeds her, changes her diaper and clothes. Puts daycare bag in car.

6:30 A.M.: Parent A and Parent B have a quick breakfast together while baby plays on playmat/sits in highchair with toy/sleeps in infant car seat.

6:45 A.M.: Parent A and baby leave for daycare drop-off.

6:45 A.M.: Parent B showers and gets ready for work.

7:15 A.M.: Parent B leaves for work.

7 A.M.–7:45 A.M.: Parent A does daycare drop-off—puts bottles in fridge, restocks baby's diaper supply, gets her settled with daycare worker, advises on how long the baby slept last night, and when her last bottle/feed was.

7:45 A.M.–4:45 P.M.: Parent B at work (with a one-hour lunch).

8:15 A.M.–5:15 P.M.: Parent A at work (with a one-hour lunch).

4:45 P.M.–5:30 P.M.: Parent B does daycare pickup and arrives home at 5:30 P.M.

5:45 P.M.: Parent A arrives home from work and takes over dinner prep while Parent B gives the baby a bath and bottle.

6:30 P.M.: Parent B is finished putting the baby to bed, and it's time for the adults to sit down to dinner.

7:15 P.M.–8 P.M.: Both parents prep the daycare bag, throw a load of laundry in the washer, clean up after dinner, and settle into some evening activities before their own early bedtime.

Of course, you can tweak this schedule as necessary, particularly if there is a long commute involved or one or both parents work at a job that requires long hours. Whatever the schedule you come up with, know that it will not last forever. If parts of the schedule are truly unbearable, consider why that's the case and see what you can do to work together to adjust it.

> ## Tip
>
> A childcare tip: break it down into bite-size chunks. Maybe a grandma doesn't have enough time or energy for watching the baby full time, but she would be thrilled to arrive at your house at 7:30 A.M. as you leave for work to feed the baby breakfast and take her to daycare.

Another Option: Designate One Parent for Each Morning

If your schedule allows, you could also designate one parent as being *on* and the other parent as being *off* on certain mornings. Again, minimalists look for time efficiency wherever and whenever possible. The *on* parent is in charge of all baby-related details for getting ready and care of the baby. The *off* parent gets to sleep in a bit or get ready for the day in a leisurely manner. If you have a later start as a family, or you have a very short commute, perhaps one parent could actually walk the baby over to daycare. The on/off morning system could also be a solution for parents to get more alone time and more time off from parenting.

Find a New Appreciation for a Working Parent's Best Friend: Sleep

Once the baby is finally asleep and your chores for the next day are done, it's so tempting to surf around on your iPad or watch just one more episode of that new television show. After all, you deserve it. You work hard, you parent hard, and you get so few hours that are truly yours. Work takes a lot of the day and the family takes the rest. You deserve to stay up till one in the morning watching a movie or organizing your bookshelves by their book jacket color. Once that precious baby is asleep, those hours stretching into midnight can be a wonderful time to recharge, relax, and have some hours to yourself.

The problem is that it's hard to shut down that *me time*. Those hours can speed by, and suddenly you find yourself up far too late. You finally get into bed, painfully aware of the alarm that goes off in just five hours—if the other alarm, your baby, doesn't go off first. In this busy world with jobs that sneak into our personal time, we are loathe to give up more of the things that we do just for ourselves, so instead, we sacrifice our own sleep.

Skip the TV. Skip the Internet surfing. Instead, go to bed. A tenet of minimalism is just keeping the best in your life, and sleep is truly the best thing you can give yourself. Some nights this will be hard. Perhaps the baby did not settle easily and was up multiple times in the early evening. He finally goes down at 10 P.M., but you haven't had any personal time. You're owed that time, right? Yes, you're owed that time for sleep. Sleep trumps all for its rejuvenating effect and health benefits. Your body requires that time to rest and rebuild. So tell yourself, when it's 10 P.M. and you have to be up in eight hours, that you will find some time for yourself tomorrow night, or on the weekend, and you will make that time count. But tonight, after the baby is finally down, you'll go to bed. This will take some willpower and Zen, when all you want to do is crash on the couch with your spouse and watch some back-to-back episodes of literally anything, but doing it will make you happier and healthier.

When you're debating what to do, remind yourself:

■   Staying up late is never worth it.

■   I will find time for myself another night.

■   Sleep is the best thing I can give myself.

If you're not getting enough sleep, as most new parents aren't, think of sleep as the most expensive and luxurious gift you can give yourself. Think of sleep as a reward at the end of the day. Think of sleep as a rare and finite jewel that you must grab whenever it appears. How's that for minimalism—you're getting back to a basic human necessity. Treat yourself with sleep!

Working Parents and Weekends

Even though your parenting duties don't stop because it's Saturday, thankfully work probably does. How can you apply minimalism to weekends? Avoid overscheduling yourself. That's no easy task when you have friends you haven't seen in months, and you hear about other parents signing up their babies for multiple weekend activities. But you'll find that leaving your schedule open makes you less stressed and more able to actually enjoy those precious weekend hours.

Keep Your Weekend Commitments Low

If you have a defined and sometimes tiring weekday schedule, try to keep your weekend free of commitments. Don't sign up for multiple baby and parent classes and don't commit to a lot of social engagements. When you have a busy weekday schedule, having a lot of white space in your weekend calendar is a good rule for limiting burnout.

Each Parent Gets a Weekend Morning to Sleep In

Split the weekend mornings so each of you gets a chance for a small sleep in and a break from morning duties. Sleeping in is a rare luxury in parenthood. There is, of course, still a baby to look after, so negotiate the sleeping-in parent's expected wake-up time in advance. If sleeping in prebaby was getting up around noon, remind each other that sleeping in postbaby, when that baby wakes up at 6 A.M. on the dot, should be more like 9 A.M. Yes, this is your new world: sleeping in until nine on a Saturday is considered a rare and much-appreciated treat. Again, the minimalist savors those few extra hours of sleep, enjoying them as a rare treat instead of bemoaning their pre-baby days of sleep abundance.

Designate One Weekend Afternoon As Chore-Free

In the same vein as creating a lot of white space on your weekend schedule, you should also designate a chunk of weekend time that is for doing nothing. No chores, no visiting grandparents, and no running to the grocery store to stock up for the week in this short window of time. You want to build in some reliable hours for just hanging out as a family, playing with the baby on the floor while you also keep an eye on the football game, having a nap together while the baby naps, and taking the time to catch up with your spouse.

> **Tip**
>
> Take a vacation day for yourself. The minimalist parent knows the value of a day spent on what were once frequent small luxuries, like a matinee movie or reading in bed for four hours. If your baby is in full-time care, treat yourself once a year to a full day off. No parenting and no work. If you want your spouse along for this luxurious day of lounging around, like you're in college and skipping classes, see if they can take a vacation day too. Having a young baby and a full-time job makes for a demanding lifestyle, so when you have a chance to cut loose with no sleep or schedule repercussions, take it.

The weeks in the first year of parenthood can both drag and speed by. You look at your baby, realize she is about to start eating solids, can roll over and sit up on her own, and then look at your spouse and realize that you haven't really talked to each other, discussed this strange and wonderful life as parents, or talked about dreams for the future in months. Sure, you can schedule a family budget meeting and you will get it done, the numbers processed, and the goals set. But those organic conversations about the future, that spontaneous play with the baby where you hear his deep belly laugh for the first time—that happens when you aren't checking things off a to-do list.

If Your Job Is Stealing All Your Time and Energy

If life is feeling impossible, and there simply are not enough hours in the day for your baby or your job, take a deep breath: you are not alone. It's very common to feel that you're not acing both parenting and work at the same time. When you feel overwhelmed, remember that this is a finite window. Babies grow up and sleep more, and they turn into children who can amuse themselves while you make daycare lunches. Soon after that, they will be in school for most of the day. Next, think about how you can simplify your schedule, outsource chores, or cut things off your to-do list. Minimalist parenting is about avoiding burnout before it sets in. So cancel that bathroom renovation, ask for an extension on a work project, or see if you can get a nanny for half the day on the weekend or arrange household help to catch up on the laundry. Think in shorter time segments, such as outsourcing or getting extra help for a brief window, either to manage a busy season—work deadlines, family commitments like a sick relative—or to catch up.

Self-Imposed Breaks from Work

Doing your best is all you can ask of yourself. Think of that when you feel like work is shortchanging your family and the family responsibilities are keeping you from doing your best at work. There is often a hard transition period for parents that have been *living the job* in the years leading up to parenthood. If you take work home with you, if you check your work e-mail as soon as you wake up, if you're always thinking about work while you're with the baby, and then missing the baby and worrying about the baby while you're at work, you need to start saying no more:

- Put your cell phone and work laptop in a box every evening from 8 P.M. onward.
- Get an old-fashioned alarm clock and stop using your phone to wake you up.
- Stop checking your e-mail before breakfast and start engaging more with your family outside of work hours.
- Think of family time and your home life as a nice break from work and work as a nice break from changing diapers and the other not-so-glamorous bits of parenting.

Set Limits with Work Colleagues

If work is creeping too much into your life at home, consider taking a more drastic action. Let your manager and colleagues know that you will no longer be available on messenger or replying to e-mails in the evening. If there is a true emergency, tell people to call you. This one step will help redefine what work is truly urgent. In this changed and busy new work world, in this age of being available at all hours of the day, we have lost those vital *off-the-clock* hours. The phrase *its quitting time* is rarely said these days. More and more jobs give you a mobile device so you feel compelled to work more hours.

Focus on the quality of your work, not how many times you answered an e-mail outside of office hours. Trying to answer an e-mail while you're giving a baby a bath is not doing either job well. Remind yourself that quality work is not done from the bathroom at a movie theater on your first date night since the baby arrived. Be focused and efficient when you are at the office, and then turn your work brain off once you're home. The work will always be there, but your three-month-old will only be this size and doing those delightful firsts, like trying to eat his toes, once.

If You Want Flexibility, Ask for It

Many parents want more flexible work hours and/or to telecommute to ease the balance with family life. Minimalist parents ask for and create flexible work situations: it's one of the best ways to manage work and family life. Some parents ask to work a forty-hour week over four days, or work from home on Fridays, or go down to a three-quarters position. In most industries, these positions are still not the norm; however, employers are listening. If you want this type of flexibility, but it's not common at your workplace, keep asking for it.

1. Start with requesting a short trial, such as working from home every other Wednesday for two months.

2. Keep a detailed record of your *wins* over the trial period, your volume of work and how it benefited your employer.

3. Once the trial is over, show your employer the benefits to them, and propose a long-term plan.

If your employer is not open or able to provide flexible work arrangements, start looking elsewhere. Progressive companies are beginning to see the advantages of offering flexible work arrangements and are using this benefit to retain great employees and lure new hires.

Your New Schedule: Stay-at-Home Parents

Being a stay-at-home parent is a challenging job: you're choosing the schedule, the activities, and prioritizing household chores with little to no outside input. It can be liberating, full of choice, and exhausting because the work often never feels done. The minimalist stay-at-home parent shirks the conventional tropes of their new title—days spent in the car driving from activity to big-box store to activity or long lonely days stuck at home—and instead finds a balance of rewarding activities, clearly defined household responsibilities, and space and time for adult interests.

Being a stay-at-home parent is truly a job. Sure, you're not being paid for it, but you would pay someone else to do all of it. Thinking of it as a job can help you set a work routine, make goals, and fight off the feeling that you're living the same day over again. It can also help you create some family routines with your spouse so you do not become the *all the time and everything* default parent. Like any job, you'll need hours off and breaks so that you can recharge, have personal time, and do great work on your hours on.

If You're Leaving the Work Force for the First Time

It's normal to have a period of adjustment to being a stay-at-home parent. This is a new identity and you may have some emotions about leaving your old identity—accountant, restaurant manager, administrative assistant, corporate warrior, teacher—behind. Most stay-at-home parents who have left careers they strongly identified with spend the first year answering the question *What do you do?* with *I used to be a _____, now I stay at home.* It's so common for people to introduce themselves with their name and their job that it can leave the newly unemployed person feeling lost.

It's okay to grieve your old identity. Even if you have plans to go back to your old job, or even if you don't, accept that you may be in an emotionally fragile state for a bit. Let yourself relax into your new role. Play around with introducing yourself and choose what greeting suits you best. Brainstorm some new ways to introduce yourself. If you like the term stay-at-home parent, run with it, but you could also say, home manager, or mom/dad, or nothing at all. You could answer the question *What do you do?* with a simple *Take care of my baby and rock Tuesday night Zumba class.*

> ### Tip
> Defining yourself by your job title is a Western construct. A work-driven culture means that we gravitate to asking about a person's job instead of their hobbies or family. In many cultures, the first thing someone may ask you about is your family, how many siblings you have, if your parents live near you, and if you see them regularly. In those cultures, family and community are how people identify themselves.

If you've been going to school and then work for a few decades of your life, it may feel very foreign and new to suddenly be in charge of your Monday to Friday daytime hours. You're your own boss now. Okay, you're your own boss with a tiny, sweet little dictator sometimes weighing in with a few demands. It's normal to have an adjustment period to this new role, and it can take time to find your groove with the baby, home, schedule, and activities. You may alternate between feeling completely overwhelmed and bored. It can take a few months, or even the first year, to find your groove as a stay-at-home parent. Let the principles of minimalism—creating white space in your schedule, using your time wisely, and sometimes saying no—guide you to creating your ideal schedule.

Routines vs. Go with the Flow

The organized taskmaster wants to schedule the day in fifteen-minute sections with naps, meals, travel time, and the biweekly church drop-in all planned out. The laid-back, nothing-on-the-books parent wants to see what the day brings instead of planning things. The happy middle ground for most parents who are home full time is a mix of scheduled activities and free time.

The overscheduled family can often push too hard and take that cranky baby, who didn't have her morning nap, to the mom-and-tot swim despite some heavy indications that it isn't a good day for it. The breezy go-with-the-flow parent may find himself or herself frustrated that they didn't register for the tumble gym class ahead of time. Now that it's full, they don't have a whole lot to occupy the cold winter day. Depending on your tendency, you'll want to take some tips from the opposite side. Either way, remember to return to the tenets of minimalism—prioritize what's most important and organize your time around those activities. By cutting unnecessary extras, you'll have less stress and more quality free time.

Ideas for Easing Into Stay-at-Home Life

Here are some ideas to help manage the transition from prebaby life to life at home with baby:

- **Have an appointment day each week.** Designate an appointment day for the week, a morning or afternoon when you always try to book medical and other appointments. It could be a time when a neighbor or grandparent is regularly available to watch the baby. Batching your appointments to one day of the week will lead to fewer disruptions in your weekly schedule and less stress about childcare.

- **Schedule household chores.** If you like to blitz the house and do four loads of laundry one day a week, designate which day that is. If you prefer to do a few tasks a day, mark off one hour a day for laundry and cleaning. Commit to this schedule as much as the baby and the rest of life allows.

- **Alternate work and fun.** Reward yourself after a morning of doctor's appointments and errands with an afternoon tea at a family-friendly café or by having a parent friend over for the afternoon and watching a movie while the babies nap.

- **Limit the stay-at-home part of the job.** Get outside. Unless you're stuck under a few feet of snow or a state of emergency has been called, try to get out of the house once a day. Everyone does better with a change of scenery, fresh air, and some socializing. For babies under one, this could be two to three planned activities a week, things you have to be at for a certain time or sign up for, and two to three unplanned activities, such as running errands, going for a long walk, or casually meeting up with other parents and babies.

- **Find the advantages of not being tied to a weekday job.** Enjoy grocery shopping when the store is empty and get those annoying errands done when shops aren't as busy. That's a great way to integrate minimalism into your day—do errands when they take the least amount of time.

- **Bring a sleeping or happy baby to a lecture.** Check out the library or any local college or university campus for a daytime lecture series or short-term class you could audit. Yes, you can be a stay-at-home parent and learn things besides teething remedies and removing banana from the carpet.

- **Join a gym that offers childcare.** Work out, sip a coffee, and read a book before picking the baby up. Even better, invite another mom friend along, hit up the noon hour pump class together, and then go for a hot tub. If you will use it regularly, a membership at a gym with childcare can be a great investment.

- **Organize a childcare swap.** Once you've found your parenting tribe, suggest setting up a childcare swap with a few stay-at-home parent friends. One day a week, that parent will leave their baby with you for two hours, and on another day, you'll leave your baby with them for two hours. You can have some alone time to get errands done without the baby along, a luxury for a stay-at-home parent, or do something for yourself.

- **Try everything once.** Try all of the free or very low-cost family fun options at least once. Check out story time at the library, the drop-in play gym at the community center, and two-dollar Tuesday family swim at least once. You'll never know if your baby will love swimming and hate the singing at the library unless you try them.

- **Go on a day trip.** Sometimes the best days are spent out of the house. Pack a lunch and snacks and head out somewhere that's out of your daily normal. If you live in a rural area, spend a day in the city, and if you live in the city, head out to a working farm, or even a suburb, that has different amenities than your area. A day trip is a great idea if you're stuck in a stay-at-home rut.

- **Take a walk.** Looking for an indoor stroll with a sleeping baby? Skip the mall and get a membership at an art gallery or museum.

- **Try something new.** Snowshoe with baby, take a baby sign language class, or spice up dinner by trying to cook authentic Thai food on a Wednesday. Decide to try something new once a week, be it an activity, a meal, or just a new route to the library.

Don't Say Yes to Everything

Now that you are home, and from an outsider's perspective have an abundance of free time, you may find yourself with a lot of requests for pitching in or taking on other people's projects. If you've gone through the exercises in this book, you've already made a list of your priorities and things that you value. Use those values to guide you to say yes or no to joining the homeowners' association, becoming the regular Tuesday driver for Great Aunt May, or hanging out at a friend's house all day to receive a nonurgent delivery. The minimalist parent can be generous with his or her time for things that matter and confident enough in those choices to say no to things that don't truly matter.

Take Advantage of Being at Home

One of the advantages of being a stay-at-home parent is that you can adjust your schedule as needed. Sick baby? Skip the morning outing and snuggle back into bed. You can get back to your routine when everyone is well. One of the perks of being a stay-at-home parent is that you're the boss and you can change the schedule on a whim. Reschedule meetings, flex work hours, and take a long lunch whenever you like. You're the boss.

Have you always said you would pursue something when you finally had the time? Now could be that time. Let those guiding values, the ones you truly prioritize above others, lead the way in choosing your new pursuit. The minimalist lifestyle is about getting rid of the *noise* and finding those few things that excite you and bring you a lot of joy. Now that you aren't tied to a forty-hour-a-week job outside of the house, you can begin to explore that distance course at the college, research starting the custom cake business you've dreamed of for years, or even train for your first half marathon. Many stay-at-home parents use naptime and evenings to work on a home-based business or study for an exam. If your secret dream demands more time, find another stay-at-home parent who wants to swap childcare regularly.

Create a Parent Network

The biggest challenge for parents staying at home can be isolation. If you're used to socializing at work, you may find yourself desperate for adult conversation when your spouse rolls in from work at 6 P.M. Long days with a baby as your side-kick can leave many parents feeling lonely, isolated, and desperate for some conversation beyond baby babble. Even the most introverted stay-at-home parents need some social time with adults to keep the balance right. Highly extroverted parents may want to put finding some parent friends ahead of getting the baby to nap in the crib.

Find your tribe at parent and baby activities or by getting enough caffeine courage to strike up a conversation with the other parent trying to settle their baby at the local coffee shop. Finding new friends as an adult is a lot like dating. You need frequent exposure to people to find out if you click and then a few one-on-one *dates* to really see if it is a match. If you don't find your tribe at one activity, try another or look online for parent meetups.

Baby milestones and antics (no sleep! exploding diapers!) change so quickly in the first year that parents often find themselves bonding with parents who have babies very close in age to their own. Strong friendships can be built over the simple commiseration of sleep deprivation and the delight over baby's first tooth. If you were in a prenatal yoga class, make sure to touch base with the members once everyone has had their baby. These types of groups can be the start of a life-long network of friendship and peer support. A lot of comfort can be found in a group like this, and it can be a great start to building a very necessary network as a stay-at-home parent.

Prioritize Baby-Free Time

The stay-at-home parent of a single child can be living the dream one moment—I just read a bestseller and ate popcorn while the baby napped!—or living a nightmare the next—I got two hours of sleep last night; I have a terrible cold; I'm wearing a bikini as underwear because we are so behind on laundry, and my spouse is traveling for work. There is a lot of joy, and some pain, to being a stay-at-home parent.

If you're a stay-at-home parent, you never leave work. This is important to note because it requires that you consciously hit the *off* switch and take a break. Schedule personal time as you would schedule seeing the dentist or getting the oil changed in your car. Make some rules that work for you and your partner: no household tasks after 8 P.M. Tuesday nights you go to book club, or on weekends, you are not the default parent. Some parents even go as far as blocking out every hour of the week and scheduling who is *on* as parent. Some parents even each take *their day* on a weekend, leaving the other parent in charge of the baby for the whole day. What may be considered strange for one family could be the key that keeps another family happily ticking along. Highly introverted parents who need a lot of alone time should negotiate a schedule that allows them to decompress at least once a week. Highly extroverted parents may need to keep a very busy schedule with lots of planned interactions with other adults. Knowing where you fall on the spectrum of needing alone time, or needing social time, will help you create a schedule that works for you.

Have Something Unusual to Look Forward To

Life with babies can feel monotonous, and it's helpful to have something out of the ordinary to look forward to. Stay-at-home parents don't have federal holidays and accrued vacation time: their job doesn't come with days off. People at traditional jobs can always take the edge off a hard day at work with the thought of their next day off. Stay-at-home parents don't get weekends away from their job or three weeks of vacation a year to reset and shake off a tough stretch at the office. If you are able to somehow book some breaks from parenting, do it. Accept the offer from a grandparent to come and watch the baby for a few days and book a mini retreat for you or you and your spouse. If you don't have the luxury of free weekday child-care, then look for low-cost or free and unusual things to do as a family, or by yourself, on weekends.

The special event to look forward to could be tickets to a concert, relatives coming for a visit, a special date night for your anniversary, or a holiday party. When you're having a rough day at home with the baby, you can find some inner peace by thinking of something on your calendar that's out of the ordinary. When that special event is over, add something else to the calendar.

Use the Semester System to Change Up Activities

Babies changes a lot in the first year. They double their weight and go from being a sleepy folded-up newborn to a crawling, food-eating, sitting-up, and laughing little being by the time they're a year old. They start sleeping less during the day and, hopefully, for longer stretches at night. Their bottles or nursing sessions tend to space out. As the baby changes, you will also want to change your weekly routine. Think of your year in semester segments, with each segment lasting for three to four months, and vary some of your weekly activities each *semester*. If you register for parent and baby classes at a community center, they often book sessions in a semester-system format with a few weeks off between semesters.

Change your activities and schedule as your baby reaches new milestones:

- The infant massage class that you started when the baby was eight weeks old will no longer be on your schedule when the baby is five months old. You'll move from activities where you sit and hold the baby to soft play activities that the baby can crawl or cruise around on.

- The group of parents you met once a week at a coffee shop will eventually move to meeting at each other's homes when the babies aren't just sleeping or feeding as you sip lattes.

- If you tried a parent and baby drop-in months ago but didn't like it, give it another chance next semester. You'll find that the groups of parents at activities change quickly. New parents come in who are on parental leave or have recently decided to stay at home. Babies grow into and out of certain activities, and if your baby was too young for the toys at one drop-in, try again when she is a bit older. Your six-month-old may shriek the entire first session in the community pool, but he may love it when you try again three months later.

Switching things up every three months is also a way to combat monotony. If you have the Monday blahs a few weeks in a row, change your schedule and try something new. If you're feeling bored with your usual routine, find something new to go to that week or revisit something you tried but gave up on. For the stay-at-home parent with no workweek breaks, a change can be as good as rest.

Changes in activity also naturally occur with a change in seasons:

- The summer may be filled with mornings at the community pool with other parents and babies, long afternoon naps at home, and evenings barbecuing in the backyard with the baby monitor on.

- Fall brings more indoor activities, registration for a class at the library, and a weekly parenting group meetup.
- Winter could involve meetups with other parents at each other's homes for a change of scenery and regularly going to a play gym that your now crawling baby can actually use.
- Spring could signal playground playdates and visits to the local zoo or arboretum.

Sample Schedule for a Stay-at-Home Parent with a Young Baby

Even though you're not rushing out the door to daycare, having a simple schedule in the back of your mind can help your days move along smoothly. Implementing some principles of minimalism in your day can also save you time and stress. For example, running an errand while you're already out will save you time getting the baby in and out of the car an extra time. Keeping some unscheduled time around naps and meals will give you a nice buffer for the often-unpredictable nature of babies. The minimalist schedule focuses on doing fewer things, but doing them better. Think of it as being specific with what and who you give your time to. For the stay-at-home parent, this may mean guarding naptime for a craft project and serving easy and simple evening meals of sandwiches, or crackers with cheese and fruit, so there's less housework in the evenings.

Use your time in ways that are meaningful and matter to you. Don't worry about your neighbor who uses naptime to deep clean her fridge or your friends who are making Pinterest-worthy Tuesday night meals. Do what's best for you.

7 A.M.–9 A.M.: Breakfast for everyone, shower for the parent.

9 A.M.–10 A.M.: Baby naps, power hour of laundry, clean one bathroom, and put dinner on in the slow cooker.

10 A.M.–noon: Activity outside the house. Library story time, baby gym time, church group meetup, meet another parent for a long walk.

Noon–12:30 P.M.: Run one errand while you are out of the house.

1 P.M.: Lunch.

2 P.M.: Naptime for baby. Parent can also take a nap, read, or have some personal downtime.

3:30 P.M.–5:30 P.M.: Indoor play with baby or out for a neighborhood walk.

6 P.M.: Dinner.

7 P.M.: Bedtime routine and dinner cleanup. Parents alternate nights for each duty.

8 P.M.–10 P.M.: Stay-at-home parent has an evening out at an activity or meetup with friends.

Again, even if you are an organizational guru who loves blocking off life in fifteen-minute segments, resist the urge to schedule your whole day or make extensive to-do lists. Babies laugh at complicated schedules and long lists of projects. Instead, create a loose schedule for your day with one or two activities and a very short list of things to get done. Make it easy to check things off your list. If you prefer to play things fast and loose and are never sure what the day will hold, start giving yourself one firm commitment each day and a short list of things to do. It could be as simple as: we're walking into town today and will get a coffee, do a small grocery shop, and dinner tonight will be chili.

> ## Tip
>
> The hours from the late afternoon and early evening are usually the hardest times of day with babies and young children. These hours are often referred to as the witching hour: babies are cranky, harder to settle, and need more hands-on help from parents. In the lead-up to the dinner hour, plan an activity or get out for fresh air to avoid the walls-are-closing-in feeling. One trick is to prepare most of dinner during the lunch hour so you can be out or focused on the baby in the lead-up to the evening meal.

Getting Back to Date Night

Once you've settled into your new routine—whatever that may be—you probably want to think about spending quality time with your partner. Your first time away from the baby as a couple will feel like you're playing hooky from school. You may giggle and run out to your car feeling free as a bird as if it were the last day of high school. Or you may feel anxious and unable to relax, check your phone constantly for messages from the sitter, leave a movie halfway through, or ask for your dinner to go because you are too worried about the baby. Both reactions, while very different, are completely normal.

It's important to prioritize time alone with your spouse once you've settled into something close to a new routine with a baby. You need that connection time that is not so readily available when there are diapers to change, breast pump parts and bottles to wash, and daycare bags to pack. Life can fill up quickly with a new baby, work, and other obligations. If you are used to a lot of one-on-one time with your spouse, you'll be surprised at how quickly a few months can go by in *baby time* with no handholding, romantic gestures, sweet surprises, or even cuddling on the couch while watching a movie. If you're in survival mode, there is little thought, or time, for loving glances and making her favorite chicken *cacciatore* on a Tuesday. One day you'll look at this person across the dining room table and think, "I remember you. I like you. Heck, I love you and want to spend the rest of my life with you; we wanted to have a baby together." Sometimes you're shoulder to shoulder getting used to parenthood and this new life for so long that you haven't had time to actually appreciate your partner.

Tip

If you have a choice for when to have a sitter arrive, ask for early. Have the sitter come at 5 P.M. and do the evening routine with the baby before putting her to bed. There are two great benefits to the early evening date. You get a break from doing those last, and often most draining, tasks of the day, and you're home early enough to get a good night's sleep. Win, win, win.

This is where your devotion to minimalism comes in. The energy you spent focusing on only what baby gear you really needed, and only on those activities you really need to do, will leave you with extra time for you and your spouse. Minimalist parents don't let the *stuff* for new babies or their home consume them—they're focused on relationships and quality time together. That means an extra twenty minutes together each night because you didn't have to pick up several boxes of scattered toys or search for that bill you lost in a huge pile of unopened mail. If you can't get out for date night and the baby is still a lot of work in the evening, try some small gestures of kindness and love to keep a bit of romance on the burner. Ask how your spouse's day went and really listen. Hold hands, even if it's while you walk around the block hoping the baby will fall asleep in the stroller. Say thank you. When one parent tackles a particularly grueling job, like emptying the diaper pail or dealing with a long middle of the night wake-up, really thank them. Small acts of kindness, gratitude, and affection can go a long way.

Once you're over the emotional hurdle of leaving your baby for a short time, try to get out regularly. For some couples, that could be a date night every other month, and for others, it might be at least once a week. Everyone is different in needs, budget, and lifestyle. If you were a homebody couple before the baby arrived, you're unlikely to become extroverts who want to be out on the town once the baby arrives.

If your budget or circumstances don't allow for hiring a babysitter, get creative. Here are several frugal ideas for getting out on a date if you don't have free babysitting from grandparents, the budget for a babysitter, or simply cannot find a suitable babysitter for a young baby.

- **Organize a babysitting swap with other parents.** Once your baby is going to bed somewhat reliably, try a babysitting swap with another family. One Saturday you'll watch your friend's baby at her house and the next Saturday your friend will come and watch your baby at your house. This not only saves you money but it can be a nice change of scenery to spend an evening at another family's home with none of your own household tasks nagging at you and, if the other baby sleeps, a few hours to yourself. Tap into the parent network you, hopefully, developed before the baby arrived or that you've built as a stay-at-home parent.

- **Have date night at home.** As soon as that baby is sound asleep in her crib, open a bottle of wine and cook some steaks together, or order in some takeout, and pretend you're at your favorite restaurant. Light a candle, dim the lights, and hide your phones.

- **Take babysitting whenever you can get it.** If your parents can only babysit on a weekend afternoon, take it. Go see a movie together, go for a long walk, or visit an art gallery. Sure, you're unlikely to see a Beyoncé concert at 2 P.M. on a Sunday afternoon, but there are still many options for exciting, can't do it with kids, date activities.

- **As a last resort, bring the baby along.** In the early days, babies sleep a lot. So if your friends invite you to an evening gathering, consider bringing the baby along. Many a couple has had an evening meal at a restaurant with a six-week-old sleeping soundly in their infant car seat beside them. People even bring little babies into quiet movies and the babies sleep soundly on a parent, in a baby carrier, or in their car seat (just be careful of the sound levels in the theater!). There is more risk involved with this date scenario. Be prepared to miss the end of a film or to be eating your restaurant meal cold and at home after having it packed up in a hurry.

Ten Ways to Simplify Your Time in Baby's First Year

- Slow down. Rip up your to-do list and enjoy all those precious firsts. To-do lists can wait.
- Cross-train each partner on all household chores and tasks before the baby arrives. You need to be able to give each other breaks and sub for one another in a pinch.
- No hosting in the first six weeks. Visitors should stay for twenty minutes at most unless they are coming over to cook a meal or do laundry.
- Split overnight parenting into two shifts. Everyone needs sleep.

- Each parent should get one weekend morning to sleep in: even if it's just until 9 A.M.
- Make date night a priority. It can be once a week, or every other month, but find time to connect with your partner even if it's just takeout pizza at home with the baby monitor nearby.
- Prep as much the night before as possible. You'll sleep better knowing the daycare bag is packed and the entire dinner cleanup is done.
- Leave as much white space as possible in your schedule. Don't overbook your weekends, particularly if both parents are working. You need downtime and room for random adult napping on the couch.
- Rethink your commute. If you have a long commute, try and find some ways to cut it. Ask to work from home one day a week or think about moving closer to the office.
- Get back to your hobbies. Even if it's infrequent and not for as long as you would like, find some time to do one or two of your prebaby activities. Leave the diaper bag at home.

About the Author

Rachel Jonat is the author of *Do Less: A Minimalist Guide to a Simplified, Organized, and Happy Life* (Adams Media, 2014) and the voice behind the popular blog *The Minimalist Mom* at *www.theminimalistmom.com*. A mother of three, Rachel's advice for living simpler with babies and children has been featured in the *Globe and Mail* newspaper, *Maclean's Magazine*, *Babble* at *www.babble.com*, and on *Today* at *www.today.com*. Rachel lives in Vancouver, Canada, with her husband and three sons in a two-bedroom condo.